How can we even begin to thank all the amazing people we met along the way? Kathy and Jim, Dale and Evelyn, Ivy and Jeff, Kerry, Vanessa and Ruby and the Blue Knights; your kindness, hospitality and friendship touched our hearts. We may have travelled thousands of miles, but it was the people we met along the way who really made the trip.

Everyone apart from the cantankerous hotel receptionist in Las Vegas! She really needs to change jobs!

All the roads we travelled, my favourite were the ones taking me back home to my family

Long Roads & Lipstick is dedicated to the memory of my parents, George and Iris. Also to my auntie Nancy, Kerry and Ruby Kurtzweg.

AUTHOR'S NOTE

"You're brave," they say. Me? Brave? I'm not so sure about that. But I do seem to have the wildest dreams! I'd like to thank my husband, Mike, for helping me believe that some can come true. This book, I hope, will inspire readers to follow their own dreams, whatever they may be.

More than anything, I hope this story will encourage my family: my children and grandchildren to always believe in themselves.

How did this all come about? A bit of a late starter to motorcycling, I gained my license at the age of 49. Then we happened to see a signpost in Canada and an idea was born.

Long Roads and Lipstick, tells the story of a journey of a lifetime with all the ups and downs, challenges and, unfortunately, some heart-ache along the way

LONG ROADS
&
Lipstick

Lynn Aitken

Lynn Aitken

CAN I CHANGE
MY MIND

A cheeky patch of deeper gravel got the better of me and I was plummeting off the road down into a deep ditch. Thinking back, I don't ever remember being scared when my bike and I parted company, just the feeling of tumbling over and over. Coming to a stop some way from my motorcycle, my mind automatically 'scanned' my body for injuries. Everything seemed OK, some pain but I was alive. Crawling over to my machine I switched off the ignition. My poor bike looked sorry for herself and I thought *SHIT!!*

That's when I got angry. Angry that I had come off, angry that I had lost control, angry that my bike was pretty damaged and angry that my panniers were strewn all over the place. But most of all, I was scared and just wanted to go home before something serious happened and I didn't see my family again. Is this trip really worth that??

Mike laughs when I lose my temper; apparently I'm a funny angry person! But he wasn't here to see this paddy; he hadn't seen me disappear into a ditch. So, how does a funny angry person have a paddy?

I picked up my wing mirror and chucked it, I picked up my indicator and chucked that and then I sat down and cried.

How must I have looked crawling up out of the embankment out of the ditch covered in dust? And, where was Mike?

Shouting and stomping my feet, "*He's left me! He's bloody left me!! Right that's it,*" I said, picking up my panniers and putting them down again, for no reason at all.

Sitting on a dirt track, in Alberta, with parts of my bike scattered around me, I thought of home. *How on earth did I get here?*

It's here, time to say goodbye. Excited? No, I'm terrified.

Being a military kid and then wife of a serving soldier, I'm used to visiting different lands and travelling. It was part and parcel of growing up, a gypsy way of life you could say. A mum and grandmother first and foremost, my fears are of leaving our family. I'm not going on a two week all inclusive vacation. Instead, my husband, Mike and I are about to ride our motorcycles from Mexico to Alaska over a period of six months.

We're leaving behind three wonderful children, a beautiful granddaughter and two lovely daughters-in-law. We would also be saying *au revoir* to my mum, Mike's mum and my aunt, who are all elderly.

Is it too late to change my mind? All Mike's planning for this trip and our bikes have already been collected by the freight company and on their way to the other side of the pond; I guess it is.

Just five years earlier, at 49 years old, I gained my motorcycle licence. Now, I was about to set out on an adventure of a lifetime. Riding a motorcycle didn't come naturally to me and I'm sure my instructor, Gordon, would confirm this, in the nicest possible way!

Living in Germany, I flew over to Scotland to do an intensive crash course, three times! Why are they called crash courses? The only time I crashed during my training was into a hedge in the school training area.

"Aye, that's the same hedge my wife rode into," Gordon said helping me get back up.

"Let's have a cup of tea," he continued.

Looking back at the dent I had made in the hedge, I followed Gordon into the portakabin for a much needed cuppa. I'm sure Gordon was as glad as me for a break! Sure enough, having that breather, I was raring to get back on the bike and try again.

With hindsight, I'm the type of person who should have learned how to ride over a longer period of time. But, I passed and I'm proud to say that I continued on to do my advanced test with IAM (Institute of Advanced Motorists) and passed first time with a *First* pass. One trait about me is that I'm determined and, I'm hoping that this will jump out at you from the pages of my book.

In the past when Mike has suggested us stopping at a well-known biker's cafe here in Scotland, it has filled me with dread. The thought of riding into a car park full of other bikers all watching us park up, still to this day, is not a pleasant thought. I'm sure it's fair to say that some bikers tend to judge other riders. Sorry guys, but it's you blokes who do most of the criticising. Checking out the *chicken strips* on another biker's tyres and forgetting that we were all learners once. In the motorcycle world, chicken strips are the part of the tyre not used. The more a biker leans over going around bends, the more of the tyre used and less chicken strips visible.

From past experience, I think female bikers are more supportive of one another and, in a group, are drawn to each other.

One of my instructors, of which I have had a few, said, *"anyone who is good at something or thinks that they are, should learn a new skill and remember what it's like to be a beginner again."*

Wise words to remember.

Anyway, that's how I came to riding motorbikes. My advice to anyone thinking about riding is, if you really want to ride, do it. But, never stop learning. Last year, Mike and I attended an IAM Skills Day at Knockhill Race Track which was incredible! Being told that you can go as fast as you like and scrape those pegs, is liberating. And, at the same time, we learnt important skills. Hopefully, I will never be the kind of rider who thinks they know it all.

So, about this trip; Mike, and I were setting off to ride from Houston to Mexico and up into Alaska starting on the 4th January 2016. Whenever I told people about the journey, the
adventure of a lifetime, I found myself wondering if I could really do this. I'm about to find out!

Mike was riding a BMW R1200 GS and I was riding my BMW F700 GS. Why do bikes have to have all these confusing numbers and letters all mixed up?

Our bikes had been prepped to go and were collected by the freight company before Christmas. The next time we would see them would be in Houston four days after we landed. Our luggage, camping kit went with the bikes, so all we had to carry on the flight was a change of clothes and our helmets. Important to keep the lids safe.

Three flights and 27 exhausting hours later, we eventually landed in Houston, Texas. It was late in the night and everything seemed very foreign, which sounds crazy as this was foreign to us, but you know what I mean!

My emotions were all over the place. Waiting for the taxi to take us to the hotel, I had to avoid looking at the Departures Board. I wanted to go home. In the taxi, my emotions got the better of me and I burst into tears. As we drove towards the lights of downtown Houston, I sobbed as quietly as I could so that the driver didn't see me. I'll never forget the concerned look on Mike's face; without saying a word, he held my hand. All his planning and I wanted to quit before we had even started. Some adventurer I was!

Jet lagged, washed out and sporting red, puffy eyes after my emotional outburst, I followed Mike into the hotel foyer. And that's when we were greeted by Sebastian, a flamboyant receptionist who wanted to chat forever and a day. Great! Just what I don't need right now. *Smile Lynn*, I told myself, even though I wanted to tell him to please just shut the hell up! And that's being polite!

I've learned so much about myself on this trip, but the first one was that a good night's sleep really does work wonders, and food, which usually means chocolate! After discovering a vending machine on our floor, I enjoyed a wee sugar fix, and promptly fell asleep.

Opening my eyes the next morning, I realised that I was famished but feeling a lot better. Did I still want to go home? Yes. Did I still want to go on this adventure? Absolutely! The relief on Mike's face was clear and, after a good hearty breakfast, we headed out to explore Houston.

Our bikes were still crated up somewhere in the UK and weren't due to land for another four days, so that gave us time to get our bearings, discover Houston and meet up with some folk Mike had been in touch with.

I've been to New York but Houston is completely different. New York, with its hustle & bustle, beeping horns and hot dog stands being wheeled up the road; yes, they really do; it's like being on a movie set. By the way, the road is called a pavement here! So if someone tells you to drive up the pavement, they haven't gone crazy. Our pavement is sidewalk here in the States which, I guess, is quite logical. It's the walkway at the side. Confused?? This is only the beginning of the trip!!

Anyways, Houston is nothing like New York. Downtown is all about businesses housed within characterless, towering structures of glass and steel. There seems to be no town centre with shops, cafes and the like. Chatting to another hotel receptionist, who was a lot calmer than Sebastian, we asked about walking to the shops. We needed a few bits and bobs from a pharmacy. *"No one walks here,"* she informed us. *"People drive everywhere or take the bus or a cab; I can call one for you,"* she added.

Taking a cab, we left the hotel armed with tourist leaflets. The cab (......it seems strange calling it a cab, so I'm going to have to go back to saying taxi) dropped us off at a pharmacy (drugstore). It also just happened to be near a camping shop and a Starbucks. Sorted! Still suffering from jet lag, the coffee and soft, chewy bagel, smothered in butter and jam, hit the spot.

The Buffalo Bayou in Houston, is a popular place for cyclists, runners, walkers and the homeless! Renting a couple of bicycles, we cycled along the Bayou looking for a well-known bat colony, documented in one of the numerous tourist flyers I had collected. This was the middle of the day and the bats would be hanging upside down fast asleep, so we just wanted to check out where it was and return at dusk to watch them wake up and fly off.

Unfortunately, we cycled the wrong way heading towards where the homeless people of Houston sleep. What a sad way to live, sleeping under bridges. The acrid smell hit us as we passed the sleeping figures under makeshift blankets. In this day and age, it saddens me to see people living like this. It also makes me realise how lucky we are.

On a happier note, and after turning around and cycling the opposite way along the Bayou, we found the bridge with the bats. The cycle was a lot nicer but nothing like the song, *Down by the Bayou*. We decided not to return to see the bats at dusk partly because we were still tired and also, we weren't sure how safe this area was.

Before leaving the UK, Mike had been in touch with Jeff Tippet from the Texas Blue Knights. The Blue Knights is an international motorcycle club for serving and retired Law Enforcement personnel. Mike, being a retired policeman and RMP, was a proud member of the Blue Knights. Mike had bought a *Drift* camera online, and Jeff was kind enough to have it delivered to his Houston address. Jeff also arranged a night out with us and a few other Blue Knights.

We enjoyed a delicious Mexican meal with the loveliest folk.

After feeling homesick and missing the family, jet lagged and unsure about the trip; it was comforting to meet up with fellow Blue Knights who gave us a huge welcome and a lot of brilliant advice for the rest of the trip.

Ivy, Jeff's wife gave me a very special calendar. The calendar features the ladies of Harley's Angels and their motorcycles.

Their motto: ***Real Women on Real Bikes Cruzin' to Cure Breast Cancer***. These amazing ladies are dedicated to promoting breast cancer awareness, research, and education. I was honoured and humbled to accept the calendar and it came with us for the rest of the trip. When you're on the road, it's easy to lose track of time; where you have been and what you have seen. It's not always easy to write a diary but a wee entry in the calendar triggers memories. Thank you, Ivy and the other Harley's Angels. The calendar came home to Scotland with me, albeit a little dustier and weathered than when Ivy gifted it to me!

Also, a huge thank you to you all for treating us to that delicious Mexican meal. I feel all warm and happy, thinking back to that evening.

HOUSTON! THEY'VE LANDED!

When people think of Houston, mostly NASA is what immediately springs to mind. So the fact that we didn't go out to NASA's flight control complex, may sound a bit strange. We thought about it but, after hearing that it was a distance outside of Houston and expensive only to say *"Houston we have a problem"* and say that we had been there, we decided that we would rather save the dosh for the rest of the trip.

They've landed!! Our bikes have actually landed. This is it. We're about to set off on an adventure of a lifetime. Leaving the comfort of the hotel, we headed off to the airport to uncrate the bikes, arrange our kit, hoping that we had guesstimated how much the bikes would carry and hit the road with our trusty (I hope) BMWs.

When my bike finally appeared from the crate, it was like meeting an old friend and a feeling of confidence washed over me; it will all be alright.

It took longer than we had thought to ready the bikes for the road and leaving Houston bang on rush hour had us changing our plans.

Crawling along the highway, nose to tail with daily commuters, we knew that there was no chance of reaching Austin that day. But that was alright as we had got no tight schedule and plans are there for changing.

Reaching a small town called Giddings, we called it a day and stopped at a hotel for the night. Our budget allowed for some hotel stops but we were hoping to camp whenever possible. The more money spent on hotels, meant less for us to spend on the trip itself.

The next day, however, we arrived at the campsite on the outskirts of Austin. The weather wasn't the warmest; in fact it was icy cold and blowing a hoolie (windy!), as we say in Scotland.

I was up for the first night camping but, when Mike saw the glamping pods and suggested we stayed in one of those, I was like *"what, really, no we can't, hell, ok!"*

Houston!

The bikes have landed!

Lipstick on. I'm ready!

That was all one breath! I'm an adventurer but I'm not stupid. I saw it as our first step to camping, ease ourselves in gently and acclimatize. The hut had a heater and television! Bliss.

Mike had booked ahead for tickets to an ice hockey match between the Texas Stars and Chicago Flyers. Unlike the Bayou in Houston, this was everything I hoped it would be and then some. The noise, the crowds, the cheering, the whole atmosphere; I loved it. Next to us, I was amazed to see a couple with a young baby, just months old.

This was a regular thing, bringing their baby to the matches. The wee one had a pair of headphones on to cut out the noise and she was quite happy watching everything. A future ice hockey player?

The next morning was a bit of a shock; there was ice on our bikes. Brrrrr! A bowl of porridge and strong coffee soon warmed us up.

To be honest, we probably would have ridden right past Langtry. If we had, we would have missed the Judge Roy Bean Visitor Centre and not met Lee!

Roy Bean was a self-appointed Judge who called himself *The Law, West of the Pecos*.

And Lee was a cheery Information Officer working at the Visitor Centre, who brought the story of Roy Bean to life.

Part Cherokee and part Scot, Lee was clearly passionate about his country and culture. When he heard that we were heading to Big Bend National Park, Lee's enthusiasm went into overdrive, and I'm glad it did!

"Wow! That's my favourite place," he beamed. It turns out that Lee's a frequent visitor to Big Bend, so not only could he tell us about Judge Roy Bean, but he also gave us hints and tips for our first national park!

The exhibition at Langtry was frozen in time with all the original buildings. Judge Roy Bean wore *two hats*, one being Judge and the other, Saloon Keeper. Roy's infatuation with British actress, Lillie Langtry, was so intense that he named his saloon, The Jersey Lilly.

The hollow thud of our motorbike boots as we walked over the wooden floorboards of the saloon, added to the feeling of being transported back in time. In those days, it would have been dusty cowboy boots.

I thought it was rather sad when I discovered that Miss Lillie visited 10 months after the Judge died. Roy never got to meet the love of his life.

We didn't make it to Big Bend in one day; instead we stayed a night in a small (and I mean small!!) town called Sanderson. Itching to try out our tent, we headed to the campsite.

"Sorry, we don't have spaces for tents," the lady apologised. I smiled, *"that's OK, no problem,"* whilst actually thinking, *what? No tent spaces in a campsite?? What strange land is this?*
Our tent, unopened yet again, we opted for a budget inn.

Texas has a new law regarding open carrying firearms. Basically, they can. To be served by a waitress wearing a loaded firearm was a bit daunting, but to hear that they didn't serve alcohol was just weird! Guns but, heaven forbid, booze! The food was lovely; basic but homemade, and if it wasn't, we weren't complaining. Fancying a wee drink, we found the town's only bar run by Julio. *Had we just walked into Moe's Bar in the Simpsons?*

Moe, I mean Julio, turned out to be an interesting and, rather eccentric chap with a big welcoming smile. Since there were no other customers, we were a captive audience for him. I was daft to ask for a glass of wine! No wine, but he had cold beer. Julio had not long retired from working with the Railroad and was in the process of setting up his bar and soon to be a grill. He was also the first of many to advise us not to travel into Mexico.

"You wanna keep your head?" he said.
Mmmm, food for thought.
We chatted well into the evening, or rather, Mike and Julio chatted. I sat and listened. I gave up talking as Julio couldn't understand a word I was saying. His expression said it all! You know, that look that says *What the hell did you just say?* Is

my Scottish accent that much broader than Mike's? Although there's not much to Sanderson, I would like one day, to go back there and see if Julio has opened up his grill.

Our first National Park in the US and our first desert! The weather was sunny and hot, just as you would expect in a desert.

But, where were the sand dunes? I'm not daft enough to expect camels in the States, but I thought that the Chihuahua Desert would have more sand! Having said that, it was beautiful nonetheless; a rocky wilderness with shrubs here and there.

When we showed our son, Daryl where we were going, he pointed to the map, saying that we were visiting a place called *Chi-hoo-ha-hoo ha!* Try saying it phonetically and you'll understand why I just had to put this bit in!!

One of Lee's tips was that we should buy an annual pass for the national parks; on arriving at Big Bend, we did just that. Costing just $80 for both of us and our bikes, a bargain! This was going to allow us free access to all the parks in the US. Although tempting to go exploring straight away, we headed to the Visitor Centre. With all the national parks, this is your best first stop. The rangers are able to tell you where to go, where not to go and all about the wildlife you're going to see. We both fancied a spot of wild camping; just us and the elements. Although it's wild camping, we still had to book at the Centre for our little bit of wilderness.

The Americans are, quite rightly, very proud of their parks and the nature that is there. Not only wishing to preserve the nature; I guess there's also the safety aspect. This is a desert after all, and if you find yourself in difficulty, there are people who know that you're there.

Our first night was in Pine Canyon. With wild camping, there are no facilities, so essentials such as the toilet involves digging a hole in the ground a small way from the tent and covering '*it*' with dirt. Before leaving, the rule is to fill in the hole with more earth.

With gusto, we headed off to the Canyon. The rangers had warned us that the five mile off road dirt track was a cheeky one, and it definitely was. Our bikes fully loaded, we stood up on the pegs and kept a forward momentum. Having completed a couple of off road courses in Inveraray, back home in Scotland, we were competent enough for this, but it was by far the trickiest dirt track we had ridden. The bikes being fully loaded made it more challenging, especially the rocky parts of the trail.

Dripping with sweat, we reached our allotted spot. On slowing, Mike hit a deep bit of sand and toppled his bike; at least the bike and Mike had a soft landing.

If anyone's going to drop a bike, it's usually me! So I felt quite useful running over to him to see if he was OK; he was and so was the bike. Between the two of us, we managed to heave the bike upright again.

What an idyllic place; no one else for miles around; our wilderness paradise, just us and nature. Pitching our tent, we cooked our tea and settled down with a couple of glasses of wine enjoying the stillness of the warm evening and watching the sun disappearing behind the rocky peaks. The sky turning a deep red before the blanket of the night takes over.
Moments such as this are what our trip is about. No distractions, no television, internet and other mod cons. *Do we miss them? Mmmmm.......no!*

Looking up at the night sky without light pollution, I was blown away with how many stars I could see. With no sun to warm the land and no clouds to act as a greenhouse, however, the night quickly turned cold. Our warm, cosy sleeping bags beckoned and we snuggled into them.

I'm not sure what time it was, maybe 2am, a loud bang woke us both up; a gust of wind had knocked over the kettle. *"I'll get it in the morning,"* I told Mike and turned over to go back to sleep.

Then another sound, this time like a train rattling down the canyon towards us. *What the?????* Before we were truly awake, it hit us; a squall like wind. Again, we thought it was just getting a bit blowy. The wind passed down the canyon; great, back to sleep. The sound of the wind seemed to be returning, travelling back up the canyon. The tent flapped wildly when it hit us a second time. Up the canyon, the squall continued. On its return, it was stronger; this repeated again and again. Crawling out of our cosy sleeping bags and out into the cool of the desert night, we checked to see if the tent was secure, only to realise that the wind was picking up strength each time; we were in a funnel!

Chatting to a Ranger the next day, he told us that this is quite a common occurrence. The hot desert airs further down, meet the cold air in the mountains and add in a funnel-like canyon such as Pine Canyon and you're in trouble!

The only option was to stay outside the tent, holding it down against the squalls; each time bracing ourselves against the wind. The extreme weather, however, forced us back inside the shelter of the awning. Holding the tent down from inside, one gust, so strong, lobbed us both across the awning along with the contents of the tent. With my head torch, I saw spiders crawling around our feet; I wish I hadn't researched, *venomous spiders in Big Bend National Park!* These little critters sharing our home looked exactly like the venomous nocturnal *Brown Recluse* spider. They were either trying to shelter from the desert storm or we had pitched our tent right on top of their nest! We were going to be bitten and die a horrible death here in Pine Canyon!! *Would anyone find us?* Of course they would as we had booked in with the rangers. Mike said (or rather shouted over the wind) that I was being paranoid but he hadn't researched this! What did he know?

"You go inside the sleeping compartment!" Mike shouted, *"Hold that part down!"*

No sooner had he said this and I was zipping myself inside the sleeping area!! No spiders in here!

"You OK out there hon?" I yelled over the wind; he replied with something but I had no idea what it was.

Mike had wrapped himself in part of the awning and covered himself with a sleeping bag to keep warm. This is how we stayed for six hours, holding the tent down until, at 8am, the wind suddenly dropped. What a dishevelled pair we looked crawling out of the tent. There was a tear in the canvas; repairable but this was to be our home for the next six months so it had to be repaired as soon as possible. There was nothing for it but to admit defeat and leave our idyllic, wild place and head to a campsite which had facilities (a shower!) and, more importantly, wasn't open to all the elements.

The ride away from Pine Canyon was, without incident, but we had mixed feelings; sad and yet, relieved. Booking in to our new campsite, Rio Grande Village near the Rio Grande river, we heard tales from other folk who had also wild camped in the canyon; all of whom had experienced the same as us. One guy informed us that his jeep had been damaged due to the winds!

Just a short walk away from the tent in our new location, were showers, a shop, a laundry and javelina wild pigs! That was nothing compared to venomous spiders! The trees, sheltering our tent, kept the heat of the desert at bay. The extremes in temperatures were incredible; scorching during the day and freezing through the night.

I couldn't help wonder if there were other folk wild camping in remote places, fighting the squalls as we had.

We spent the rest of the week in Rio Grande Village; this was our base while we explored Big Bend; Mike also managed to repair our tent.

Much of the time here, was spent hiking and exploring the park. We had chosen the right time of year to visit, as the, already, high temperatures, soar even more during the summer months and us Scots would have found the intense heat too much to enjoy any activities at all.

One of the hikes was the *Lost Mine Trail,* high in the Chisos Mountains; Big Bend has a wild, but arid beauty. Would I go back there? I was glad that we went there but I wouldn't return; distances between places in the park are quite vast and the ride between, boring, with signposts counting down the miles!

Big Bend is on the border to Mexico, with the Rio Grande River acting as a natural border line. Our first visit to Mexico was taking the international boat (a rowing boat) over the Rio Grande to Boquillas; a village seemingly existing entirely for the tourists from the US side.

On the Mexican side of the Rio Grande, we rode a couple of donkeys into the village, led by a guide. We didn't ask for a guide; but weren't given a choice; deciding not to question this, we followed our guide, who didn't speak English, around the village. Unsurprisingly, he took us to his home to meet his wife who tried to sell us her wares. When it was time to ride the donkeys back to the *ferry,* we thanked our guide and tipped him. He didn't look happy and complained that we hadn't tipped him enough; that much we understood! Reluctantly, I handed him a bit more; my thoughts were that it was probably best to just pay up and leave!

A visit to the hot springs by the Rio Grande River was a relaxing one, as well soothing our tired muscles after riding. The river isn't as wide as I thought it would be but, remembering back to the old western movies, cowboys used to ride over the river to escape the Mexicans, or, I guess, and vice versa.

I consider myself a positive person; every cloud has a silver lining and all that. Our silver lining after the storm and having to flee to Rio Grande Village was meeting Kathy and Jim Weir from Tucson. Sitting in the laundry room checking our emails, (only place with wifi), with other folk doing exactly the same, conversation started flowing. You'll meet Kathy and Jim again further in the book. Suffice to say that we met two wonderful, kind people who will be friends for life.

I'm not sure how Big Bend got its name as there's nothing bendy about the road leaving the national park. Long, straight and boring, but the only way is forward to get anywhere.

International ferry across the

Rio Grande River to Mexico

FRONTIER POSTS & MADDOGS!

Passing little towns such as Alpine, which wasn't alpine as we know it, and Marathon, we soon arrived in Fort Davis. There's Fort Davis, the small town and Fort Davis, the frontier military post which was active from 1854 to 1891. Today, the fort is preserved as a reminder of daily life during the development of the western frontier.

I would much rather visit places like Fort Davis than read about them in a book. Standing in the very spot where the soldiers and families worked and lived, really brings it to life. The fort was in an ideal place; a box canyon, close to water, wood etc; but standing there in the heat looking up at the crags surrounding us, I could imagine Apaches on their horses appearing on the ridge line. We would be learning a lot more about the Indians, the First Nation; one of them being that the Apaches were raiders and fighters.

Escaping the heat, we headed into the Visitor Centre at Fort Davis, ready to pay our entry fee, only to discover that this was part of the National Park Service, so we were able to use our annual pass.

After visiting the fort, we wandered around town looking for somewhere to eat. Coming across a small, rough and ready cantina called Maddogs with a tree growing through the roof, we both looked at each other, wondering whether to go in or not. Where to eat was still unknown territory to us.

In Europe, we kind of know what to expect, and Maddog's

would probably be the sort of place best avoided. But, what the hell!

The food was homemade and delicious and they catered for *bad hunters* (vegetarians...me!)

Waiting on our food, what we thought was a painter/decorator came and sat at the table next to us. Chatting to this most interesting chap, he turned out to be Maddog himself and the owner of the cantina. Maddog had lived for a time in Munich so we had a blether in German.

Happy that we had decided to eat there, on the way back to the hotel, we stopped at a Bistro for a glass of wine where an abrasive lady behind the bar, served us. The Bistro was fancier than Maddog's but don't judge a book by its cover....the wine was nice, the service was awful and looking around at folk eating, the food didn't look as tasty as we had just eaten at Maddog's.

High above Fort Davis, in the mountains, is the McDonald Observatory. We shouldn't miss it, we were told whilst in Big Bend. Not being on a strict time frame, there was no reason not to visit the observatory, and we are truly glad we did. Just as the sun was setting, we dressed warmly and rode the scenic way up into the mountains; truly magical.

We were off to a Star Party at the Observatory! Using a laser pen pointed at the night sky, the astronomer brought the constellations to life in the form of mythological creatures, animals and people.

This was followed by the chance to go around the various telescopes and view star clusters, nebulae and the surface of the moon. Are we really alone in this vast universe?

The border town of Presidio, the last stop before crossing over into the unknown! I was still feeling nervous about travelling into Mexico; we had received a mixed bag of advice, some telling us that we could lose our heads, whilst others saying that it's a magnificent country to explore. One such person was an American chap who we had met in the hot springs back in Big Bend.

After telling him our concerns, his response was, *"sure you have to be careful but that's anywhere. The drug cartels do run Mexico but their parents, uncles, aunts, own the hotels, restaurants, bars where the tourists go. They're not going to jeopardize their family's businesses by scaring the tourists away. The violence is usually between the different drug cartels and you would have to be unlucky to get caught up in it"*

That was it; our minds made up. Thank you Mr American guy; sorry we didn't catch your name. Yes, we're going to Mexico.

Stopping in a motel for the night; there's not much I can say about that. I was at a bit of a low, missing the family and home. Desperate to stretch my legs but nowhere really to walk, I trekked along a dusty road for a while and back again! Walking along with the sun beating down on me, my mind wandered to home, *what the hell am I doing here?* I asked myself.

Shaking off the dust back at the motel room, Mike asked, *"Was that a nice walk?"*

"Absolutely," I lied, knowing full well that Mike knew that as well.

Opening my eyes the next morning, I was feeling a lot better and ready to take on Mexico! This was going to be interesting, crossing the border; *was it going to be straightforward or are we going to be stuck for hours in the heat?* I wondered.

Wow, how easy was that? Having the right paperwork was the key to our problem free crossing.

Ojinaga seemed a bit of a crazy, border town and all my senses were on high alert! In my head, I didn't see people going about their own daily routine; I saw gun toting, axe wielding drug lords ready to cut off our heads if we didn't hand over our cash! You're either thinking, *Woah, these two are crazy for going across the border!* Or, *she needs to get a grip!*

Still nervous about being in Mexico (do ya think??); I could see Mike slowing down looking for a cash machine. He must have felt the vibes from me following behind urging him to keep going. There was no way I was going to stop in a border town.

After surviving crossing the border and the ride through Ojinaga, we arrived in Creel, a town in the Sierra Tarahumara in the State of Chihuahua. Tourists flock here each year to visit Copper Canyon; a series of six canyons which, together, is four times bigger than the Grand Canyon. This part of Mexico is also home to the Rarámuri or Tarahumara people who, still to this day, wear their traditional multi-coloured clothes.

Being at high altitude and still early in the year, the temperatures were lovely and warm during the day, but down to minus 6 at night. With this in mind and being wary about camping here, we opted for a cabin. Glamping again.

Time to give our *ponies* a rest; we hired a couple of bicycles to explore the area around Creel. My bike, though, had no gears and had a weird, bouncing motion which was amusing to start with but that was short lived when my butt started complaining; oh for a pair of those padded cycling shorts!

Cycling through the Valley of the Monks with the towering natural rock formations, I wondered why it was called this. I couldn't see any monks. The Valley of the Mushrooms and the Valley of the Frogs, on the other hand, were both obvious names for the rock formations found there. So I did a bit of research. The Valley of the Monks was originally named Bisabirachi Valley by the Tarahumara Indians. This literally meant, *Valley of Erect Penises*, but it was re-named so as not to offend anyone. I, personally, prefer the original name.

Cycling around this bizarre, otherworldly land, we passed by caves where the Tarahumara still called home. I had the feeling that we were intruding, a bit like peering in through someone's windows. These proud and private people are wary of tourists but seem to accept that this is the way of life now. We cycled by respecting their privacy. There was one cave, however, where the occupants invited us in for a small price. We were amazed at how modest and basic their way of life was; definitely no internet here!

The family living here, smiled at us in a shy reserved way. Their home was perfect for the climate, offering shade and cool in the summer and cosy in the winter. In fact, they had everything they needed, basic as it was, and no stresses or distractions, such as television. *Did they even know who Trump was? I wondered? Who was really better off? What would Mike say if I suggested getting rid of the television?* Then, I remembered what happened when I did.

The children were young and I had started Tai Chi with all the meditation and tree hugging; no, seriously, the class I attended, occasionally hugged trees!!!

The kids were at school; Mike was at work......perfect. I removed the television and, in its place, created a Feng Shu area instead. I proudly showed the family my creation; mutiny!!

"*Where's the tv?*" Mike and the children asked in horror.

"*It's been put away for the time being,*" I replied, "*we're going to have more family time,*" I added confidently.

Their faces said it all and needless to say, I lost and the television was hauled back out from the cupboard!

Most destinations in Mexico such as the Cusarare Falls mean that going off road is a must. The Mexican roads, on the whole, were OK and constantly being improved, however, sometimes the tarmac just stops and you're back to dirt or worse, gravel. In the UK, we complain about potholes; I will never complain about potholes again! Some of the potholes in Mexico really have to be avoided; and what about the topes? Topes are equivalent of our speed bumps, brutal ones at that; and unmarked so invisible until you're going over one! Even the two speed bumps going into work at Scone Palace aren't a patch on topes!

Not being able to find a tarmac road to Cusarare Falls, we quite happily turned onto a dusty track. Again, I was glad that we'd been on the off road courses in Scotland before we embarked on the trip.

After a kilometre down a bumpy, stony dirt track, we

couldn't go any further, so, under the watchful and amused eye of a Tarahumara family, we parked the bikes, changed into our walking clothes and set off on a 3km walk through an idyllic pine forest following a dry river bed.

On arriving at the falls, we saw a couple of coaches parked up with tourists disembarking.

"*So,*" I said to Mike, "*looks like there is another road to the falls!*"

Having said that, I preferred the route we took; we were able to experience the beautiful pine forest. The tourists on coaches are driven around, dropped off to see the sights and hop back on the bus for another quick stop off; all to a tight schedule. You can guess which way Mike and I like to do things; not the easy way, but oh so much more interesting.

Near to the falls were the Tarahumara women weaving their baskets and trinkets for selling to the tourists. All natural with no plastic. I don't usually buy tourist souvenirs, but I would have liked a woven basket from these proud people, but we just didn't have the space on the bikes.

The waterfall itself wasn't gushing with water; in fact, it was still partly frozen. Winter had suspended the water in its downward course over the falls. Now spring was here and the warm sun was melting the ice, only to freeze again overnight. Although not a roaring, cascading waterfall at this time of year, Cusarare Falls was still spectacular. I can only imagine how amazing the falls would be in the wet season. Standing at the foot having the obligatory photograph taken, a large chunk of ice broke off and nearly landed on my head; time to go.

Going on this adventure was a huge step for me. Mike made this trip possible and I trusted his decisions completely. Batopilas, though, was one place too far. A former silver mining town, Batopilas sits at the foot of Copper Canyon. The newly surfaced road makes the four hour trip to Batopilas easier than it once was.

I wouldn't have minded the journey; I like a challenge. However, to hear that some children of Batopilas are running around with guns and ammunition slung over their shoulders was something I had no desire to witness. I have a family back home and I wanted to return to see them again.

Chances are the visit to Batopilas would have been an amazing one and without incident, but I didn't need to take that risk.

"Just think, though. Going to a Narco town will make for interesting reading in your book," Mike suggested. He had missed the point though; this book is about the whole picture. The trip's amazing but pales into insignificance compared to my life back home with my family; so, no Batopilas, I'm afraid.

We, in the UK, are a nation of animal lovers, so to see stray dogs running around looking for scraps of food was, for me, heart-breaking. I'm such a softie and took to buying sachets of dog food to feed the strays. The folk of Creel gave me strange looks and must have thought that I was a crazy European, which I admit, I am!

Mike saved the fat from his steak one night and I offered it to a poor hungry looking pooch. The dog took to his heels, tail between his legs, thinking I was crazeee as well. Another hungry dog wasn't so nervy and enjoyed the feast.

One evening, we were aware of a commotion going on outside in the Creel dog community; the barking and yapping coming from all directions. Upon leaving the restaurant, we realised that there wasn't a dog to be found. Later on, we found out that the Creel Town Council gather up the stray dogs every now and then; where were they taken? No answer to that question; feeling sad, I suddenly had a thought; *was that beef Mike's been eating?*

We may think that our lives are so much more sophisticated, but there's a lot we could learn from these proud people of Creel. I saw people living in makeshift shacks for want of a better word, but they have their traditions and values that we, in our *sophisticated* lives, may have lost sight of.

What am I talking about? Fruit and vegetables! What??? Has she gone completely mad?
This is a message to our big supermarkets and you know who you are! Why do our fruit and vegetables have to be wrapped in plastic? What is going to happen to my turnip if, heaven forbid, it has no plastic cling film on it? This trip is not just about the places we visit but also to experience different cultures and ways of life.

Although this is a big adventure, we still have to shop for food; we need to eat. It occurred to me, one day in a Mexican supermarket, that the fruit and veg were all different shapes and sizes and unwrapped. And they tasted delicious. OK, that's my rant over.....for now.

Leaving Creel, we headed towards our next destination; Yécora. The road was full of twisties; a great road for biking and one of the best we experienced on the whole trip.

Riding defensively is a must in Mexico; the yellow lines down the middle of the road don't mean anything. We weren't surprised to take a bend and find a truck on our side of the road.

Some of the potholes were so deep and sudden that going into the wrong one could have had us off our bikes. So that's avoiding the oncoming trucks and the potholes. Anything else? I forgot to mention the ice didn't I?? Going over the hills and at high altitude, that, as well as the time of year, meant that ice melting off the hills during daylight hours running over the road, was freezing again through the night. One path of ice covered the width of the road and we just rode forward and hoped for the best! There was nothing else for it.

The town of Yécora sounds exotic and yet, in reality is a sad looking place. Straight away I was relieved that we were only here for one night. Down on its luck, Yécora definitely wasn't a tourist destination but that's not why we're here. This is us experiencing the real Mexico. There's a lot of poverty and not a lot of money to improve things. We found a dingy hotel which wasn't as clean as I would have liked but it was for one night only; I slept on top of the bed in my sleeping bag though. Looking at the shower and the walls covered in mould, I decided that I really didn't need a shower that night! The wind was howling when we left Yécora, blowing the sand up into the air and straight at us. The road, as usual, full of potholes, but we were used to them by now and getting pretty good at avoiding them.

Riding high up into the hills, the views were breathtaking. The landscape in Mexico is diverse and stunning, and thinking back to the typical tourist destinations, I wonder how many visitors venture further than the complexes with the bars and swimming pools and discover the real Mexico; warts and all.

Our next destination was Baja which involves taking the overnight ferry from Topolobampo. Still too early, we thought we would be organised and buy our tickets at the Baja Port before heading into nearby Los Mochis for a meal. The system was an interesting one which was duplicated unnecessarily, but who are we to criticise the way they do things?

Riding one at a time onto a weigh ramp, the bikes were

weighed, paying 50 Pesos each for this. The paperwork was then checked by another person before buying our tickets in the main office. Where's the duplication? You'll see later on. Apart from this, however, the total cost of the crossing including our cabin, was approximately £200, which, I thought, wasn't too bad.

THE CALL FROM
HOME

Having enjoyed a meal in the town of Los Mochis, we were in good spirits and heading back to the bikes when we received a heartbreaking call from our daughter, Hazel, who was back home in Scotland. This amazing trip suddenly meant nothing; we wanted to go home; our daughter needed us. I may talk about this later on and I may not, but it was serious. In Los Mochis, we didn't know just how serious until later on. Our son, Daryl, his wife Kim and our granddaughter, Dharyl, who live in Thurso, jumped in the car and drove through the night to be with Hazel. Vaughan, our older son and Lacey, his wife, were living in Cyprus; Vaughan was also planning on heading home.

With all enthusiasm for the trip gone and not knowing what to do for the best, we rode back towards the ferry. Here comes the duplication; we had to do the whole process of the weigh ramp again and pay again. A good idea to have loose change handy; we were getting used to the Mexican way of things.

Standing in the queue by our bikes, waiting to board and with heavy hearts, we hugged each other, shedding tears. This was going to be a long night.

Hindsight is a great thing, but on reflection, I should have done what I wanted to do and ride to the nearest airport, park the bikes and go home to our daughter; one of the biggest regrets in my life.

Finally we boarded the ferry onto the car deck; Mike had kept the tie down straps from the freight company just in case the Mexican ferries didn't provide them. He was right; there were no straps. Unfortunately they directed us to part of the car deck with no anchors; redundant straps!!

"Is OK, no problem, bikes will be OK," the car deck attendants promised.

OK, when in Rome, I mean Mexico!

Worrying about Hazel, also about Daryl driving through the night to Stirling: we felt helpless. We could only try and catch some sleep and get somewhere with Wi-Fi as soon as we got off the ferry in the morning.

During the night, the ferry began rolling and lurching; the Sea of Cortez was stormy, rough and angry. *How are the bikes riding out the storm untethered,* I wondered.

The next morning, our hearts sank at the sight of our bikes lying on their sides. The car deck attendants saw us and came running over to help us pick them back up. Back upright, Mike started waving his arms about and protesting to the men. Speechless, the attendants apologized and, sheepishly, walked off away from the crazy arm flapping Scotsman.

It took two hours to disembark, and with every minute that passed, I was desperate to get to somewhere with internet access. Before this, though, more checks, this included import documents and paying Import Tax. Then another inspection, this time, our passports, and finally the military check. There are a lot of military checkpoints dotted throughout Baja and usually fairly straightforward. The soldiers were always interested in where we were from and where we were heading to.

It was lunchtime by the time we reached La Paz; the first opportunity to call home. Straight away I liked this touristy pretty seaside town. It was clean and vibrant; a surfer's paradise. Although being lunchtime, we needed breakfast and to call home. Sitting with a plate of food in front of me, I realised that I didn't feel hungry.

I was just relieved to finally be able to talk to our family and, although, a lot of tears, we knew that Daryl was now in Stirling and looking after Hazel. Vaughan had managed to book a flight home to be with his sister. Just ten miles from leaving his house in Cyprus, his car broke down on the way to the airport and he missed the flight; his heart, however, was in the right place.

I was, in a way, relieved that Vaughan hadn't caught the flight as this was only as far as England and he was planning on renting a car to drive up to Scotland. I would have been worrying about him.

Heading away from La Paz, we were soon riding through barren countryside; I felt so far from home at this point and my thoughts were all about how I could get a flight home. In a way, I think I would have felt happier staying in La Paz that night. Civilisation was good at the moment and we were riding further and further into a wilderness; at least that's how it felt at that moment.

This was the closest we came, on the whole trip, to running out of fuel. Riding towards San Ignacio, we had checked on Sat Nav where the petrol stations were so we could calculate the distances we could ride between fuelling up.

Riding into the first petrol station, our bikes weren't desperate for fuel. Just as well, as there was no way the run down and derelict petrol station was open. That was fine; the next chance to get fuel was not too far away; wrong! Riding into the next station, it was open but, unfortunately, not for gas! A makeshift sign read, 'No Gas.'

Doing the maths, we weren't sure if we could make it to the next one; but there was nothing for it but to try. Riding conservatively, we ate up the miles and watched the fuel gauge go down. By the time we reached the next station, the bikes were running on fumes. Yes! It was open and had fuel! Mike filled his 20 litre tank with 20.4 litres! Note to self; don't rely on sat nav and top up whenever we could.

Taking two days of riding through the desert, we suddenly found ourselves in the balmy oasis town of San Ignacio surrounded by date palms. Ancient trees around the town square provide a leafy umbrella of shade from the hot sun.

Just 59 kilometres from this small town is San Ignacio Lagoon and the winter sanctuary and breeding waters of the gray whales, and that's why we were here; to see these majestic creatures. But first, set up camp in the *Rice & Beans campsite.*
What a lovely name for a Mexican campsite. Later on, I thought it should have been called, *Rice, Beans and Margaritas Campsite!*

The site itself was quite basic and the cleanliness of the toilets questionable, but having heard about the margaritas they served here in the bar, we just had to give it a go. Being a wine girl, margaritas isn't a drink I have tried, that was until Baja! Wow!! And that was just watching the drinks being made. Then the taste; oh my days; it was served in a large bowl like glass; the taste, delicious and refreshing. I didn't realise how strong Ricardo's margaritas were and the first drink went down way too quickly. By the way, that was Mike's thoughts, not mine! I was fine, but I did sip the second glass more slowly; we were there for a week so I had to learn to pace myself.

One balmy evening, walking down to the supermarket, we passed the bus terminal on the way. This evening, the terminal was being used as both a bus station and funeral parlour. A group of people were gathered around the open coffin with the deceased on show for the mourners and passengers. I couldn't tell who was who! Silly of me to think that, in Mexico, a funeral parlour would be anywhere else than in the local bus station!

We have met some interesting people on this trip already and I can't forget to tell you about another unforgettable character, this time, a furry, four-legged spaniel (ish) we named Sandy. Constantly wagging her tail and visiting the campers, Sandy played on her cuteness! This dog was a survivor and was probably the best fed dog we had seen in Mexico. Mike was smitten with this fluffy ball of fur and couldn't resist feeding her. I don't know where she slept at night, but she was by our tent each morning waiting for her breakfast.

Waking up and popping my head out of the tent, I was thrilled to see that the weather was perfect for our whale watching experience. Tickets bought for the boat trip, we made our own way to San Ignacio lagoon. After 48 km of paved road, the tarmac abruptly stopped and the last 12 km was a mixture of washboard, dirt track, gravel, sand and rocks. Standing on our pegs, we arrived at the lagoon, shaken but not rattled.

The shallow waters are a safe haven and perfect nursery for the gray whales to give birth and feed their calves. We were a bit uneasy about going out and potentially disturbing these beautiful animals, especially when they have their young with them. Our fears were unfounded as the lagoon is 36 km long and 6 km wide and the small tour boats are restricted to a tiny part.

The whales, for whatever reason, seem to like human interaction and approach the boats willingly.

What a breath-taking and beautiful experience; I could hardly believe that we were seeing these gentle giants of the deep. Not just one or two, we could see literally dozens of whales and their calves. In every direction we looked, there were whales. Most were swimming peacefully, but occasionally and unbelievably, a playful whale would breach the surface, into the air splashing back down and disappearing beneath the waters.

It wasn't long before we were approached by mums with their calves. They swam alongside our boat unperturbed by human spectators and seemed to enjoy an invisible connection with us. The whales swam so close, in fact, that we were covered in whale snot! I was in awe, I felt humbled and was speechless, even with whale snot on me; what an honour.

How can I follow that up? Oh yes, I remember. We both ate sand! On a high and feeling energised after seeing the whales, we rode away from the lagoon. I followed Mike over the washboard, cheeks rattling......both sets! Unfortunately Mike spotted some smoother sand to the side of the washboard. We soon learned the hard way that smooth sand means deep sand. We should have kept to the hard washboard. Mike came off his bike first, followed by me. Sand gets everywhere, especially when you dive into it, mouth open! Spitting out sand, we picked ourselves up, dusted ourselves off and checked our bikes. Thank goodness our landing had been a soft one; our bikes were fine, albeit a tad dusty. My BMW Vario panniers (sorry BMW!!) popped off as soon as the bike hit the ground. Mike's panniers which aren't BMW, stayed intact.

It was time to pack up the tent, say goodbye to wee Sandy and continue our travels. As we ruffled Sandy's furry head, she spotted another happy camper preparing breakfast; without looking back at us, she toddled, tail wagging, looking oh so cute. So long and thanks for all the food! Bye Sandy.

Heading north up through Baja, we stopped overnight in an oasis village called Catavina. There's not a lot to Catavina, apart from an oasis, a hotel, a small settlement and giant rocks. We opted for staying in the hotel, which, being the only place in town and surrounded by desert, travellers are caught by the short and curlys with, the price they charge for rooms, reflecting that.

Having recovered from the price of our stay, we hiked up the dusty tracks on the outskirts of Catavina, climbing over a boulder field to a point where we could sit and gaze down seeing the village in its entirety. It was humbling to see how the locals lived here compared to the plush hotel, with some houses put together with plywood. I felt bad about staying in a nice hotel while there were folk living in obvious poverty, but I also realised the hotel is providing much needed employment for the villagers.

Each day riding north meant we were closer to leaving Mexico and crossing back into the USA. We had one more overnight stop before crossing the border, this time in Ensenada. This bustling touristy town with a busy port is an attack on all the senses especially after the hush of the desert. Just 68 miles to the border crossing at Tecate, we booked into a hotel for our last night in Mexico. Being a tourist destination, the hotel wasn't cheap or 'inexpensive' as my father-in-law preferred to say. The hustle and bustle of the fish market and the different aromas coming from the restaurants, along with the chatter of folk enjoying the balmy evening, was an enjoyable and
memorable end to our Mexican experience. Would I come back to Mexico? Perhaps, but I'm not sure. There are so many other destinations in the world to discover.

The small town of Tecate is meant to be a calmer crossing than the busy port of Tijuana and also home to Tecate beer, one of the most popular beers in Mexico.

It was a scorching hot day by the time we had reached the border crossing. Wearing bike kit on a hot day wasn't a problem until we weren't riding anymore. Not sure where we were meant to go, we sat on our motorbikes, looking all around us. I could feel the sweat trickling down my back; finally we realised that, to get our paperwork checked and stamped for crossing into the US, meant going to two different offices. No problem there other than the offices were two miles away from each other! The necessary done, the actual crossing took just minutes and we were back in the US of A. Next stop; El Centro.

So, El Centro is taking more than its fair share of the sun!!! Are we bitter in Scotland? Definitely not; our soft rain makes good whisky and we have a lot of whisky, so you can probably imagine how much rain we get! Maybe a little bit more sunshine would be rather nice though.

It was quite easy to find a campsite which would accept a tent and we were the only people camping. This park was full of static caravans, Canadians escaping the harsh winters for the sun; a nickname for them is *snowbirds*. Of all the campsites we have stayed in, the one in El Centro was by far the most luxurious.

I love the simplicity of life on the road but when there's a hot tub on offer, I'm right there! Better still, campers, or rather caravaners, tended to go to bed early, giving us the hot tub to ourselves. Soaking in the warm, bubbling waters and looking up at the stars and the occasional plane flying overhead, again my thoughts were of my family.

There's a reason the campers go to bed early, it's to get up bright and breezy at 6am for a round of golf! And where was our tent, but right by the golf course!

It wasn't just the golfers that woke Mike up. Sand flies had chomped away on Mike's feet whilst camping in San Ignacio and the red itchy spots were raised and looked infected.

"*Yuck, they look infected!*" I said screwing up my nose. I've got a good bedside manner, you can tell!

"*You need to see a doctor,*" I added more sympathetically.

It was a Saturday, but we found a *Walk In* clinic fairly close to the campsite.

After telling the receptionist the problem, she asked "*Have you had a colonoscopy?*"

To say Mike looked shocked was an understatement.

"*I want them to look at my feet, not the inside of my arse!*"

"*Stay calm Mike,*" I said, "*They know what they're doing.*"

This was going to be interesting!

No colonoscopy this time! Mike's arse remained intact. The doctor examined Mike's bites and sent him away with lotion and antibiotics if it turned nasty.

THE TALE OF TWO SHOES

Leaving El Centro took longer than we had planned. It was a Sunday which meant phone calls home to the kids which I always looked forward to. Before leaving Scotland, we took out an added 'extra' on our mobile phone contract which meant that, for £5, we could have a day's unlimited phone calls home one day a week.

Then saying goodbye to the happy campers took some time; they were a friendly bunch of people. At last, though, we were on the road again.

After a few miles on the interstate, glancing in my wing mirror, I realised that my roll bag had opened slightly and something went flying out of it. I rode past Mike, signalling to stop. I couldn't believe it; I had lost one of my Merrell walking boots. Gutted! These boots had walked the West Highland Way with me.

"*What's wrong?*" Mike asked when we stopped at the side of the road.

When I told him about my boot, Mike took my other boot out of the roll bag and lobbed it away. "*We can't go back and one shoe is no use,*" he said.

Fixing my holdall firmly shut, we headed off again.

It's only a shoe, I thought, *I could buy a pair of trainers for the rest of the trip*, at the same time, still feeling quite sad and sentimental.

Another couple of miles further along, Mike was the one who was signalling to stop. He had just realised that he had left his bum bag back at the RV Park. For our American readers; fanny pack!

The bum bag had passports, money, pretty much everything we needed.

There was nothing for it but to turn around and ride the 17 miles back to, hopefully, retrieve his bag. On the way back to El Centro, I spotted my first lost boot on the other side of the interstate. Taking note of its position, I thought that I may just get my pair of boots back again.

Luckily, Mike's bag had been handed in to the reception and I excitedly told Mike about my boot. This time, Mike followed me out of El Centro and a few miles later, I saw my shoe. Mike remembered where he had chucked my other one so off we went again. Another few miles later, we found my other boot. Seeing my shoe lying on the road, I noticed, for the first time, that I have tiny feet!

Happy to have my boots and mike's bag back, we headed off again.

Leaving El Centro, California, we headed east towards Tucson, Arizona. I admit to not knowing much about Arizona before but now, looking back, I think it's fair to say that this was my favourite State.

Situated in the Sonoran Desert, Tucson is surrounded by five mountain ranges. Historically, Tucson was an Indian village called Stook-zone, meaning *water at the foot of Black Mountain*.

I'm sure a scientist would be able to tell me why Arizona has the most jaw dropping, beautiful sunrises and sunsets, but the science would be lost on me. For that brief moment each day, we watched the desert skies ablaze with deep oranges and reds.

In Scotland, we quite often have lovely sunrises and sunsets. The sun says *"hello"* and *"night night,"* and in between, the weather is shite! But, our men folk wear kilts and no pants! Real men or just plain stupid???

The lovely couple we had met in the laundry room in Big Bend National Park, Kathy and Jim, live in Tucson. We were going to meet up with them again. Kathy had invited us to stay with them but I'm a bit shy about staying with people so we, or rather I, decided to set up camp and we would spend a few days with Kathy & Jim.

Our first outing with them was for a meal and I knew then, that Kathy and Jim were going to be friends for life. We just clicked; it was as if we had known them for years. Tucson happened to have a BMW dealer which we needed to visit for a little repair job on my bike. After my bike toppled over on the ferry crossing to Baja, my brake light was permanently on; something just needed tweaking.

After dropping my bike off at the garage, we headed to the shops. Before we could enjoy any touristy sightseeing, I needed new knickers and a blouse; I'm a lady of few needs and considered low maintenance by Mike. I may need to address this once I'm home!

Our campsite was surrounded by desert and cacti. The reason I needed a new blouse, was due to me walking near the Cholla cactus which launched fine spores at me. A walking pincushion, the spores were so fine that I had to ask Mike to pull them out of me using a tweezer. It was impossible to get all the spores out, so my blouse was ruined. At first, I thought that a tarantula had attacked me! Ever the drama queen and such a tourist!

The Sonoran Desert in Arizona has an array of cacti; from towering majestic *Saguaro* with multiple 'arms' to the ground hugging *Golden Barrel* cactus. Fascinated by the variety of cacti growing all around us, I wanted to find out more about them.

Kathy's knowledge far exceeds any tourist guide books I could buy; I listened intently.

"See here, this is the prickly pear cactus; the fruit makes delicious jelly and margarita," Kathy said smiling. With fond memories of the margaritas in Baja, *Oh, I might just have to try that,* I thought.

"What's that one, Kathy?" I asked, pointing to a low lying spiky plant with one tall flower stalk growing from the centre

of the cactus.

"*That's an Agave,*" Kathy explained, "*the flower means that it's going to die,*" she added.

This was the monocarpic Agave which flowers once in its lifetime and then dies. Looking at the flowering cactus, now knowing that it was going to die, made me feel slightly sad.

"*It should be called 'the swan song' cactus,*" I suggested.

Whenever I saw a flowering agave, I took a moment to admire the plant's final dance.

Kathy pointed to a dry, unassuming twig like plant; "*That's an amazing plant,*" Kathy said.

On seeing my bewildered expression, Kathy smiled, "*it's called a Night-blooming Cereus, or another name is 'Queen of the Night',*" she continued.

Kathy has one of these plants in her garden; one balmy evening when the Cereus was going to bloom, she used time lapse to film the entire *performance.*

Showing me the footage on her phone, I watched in amazement, as night fell, the small bud slowly opened revealing a beautiful large white flower. The white flower dazzles against the dark skies; its scent, enticing moth to feed and pollinate; the bloom dies before the sun's hot rays touch it.

Donning my new blouse, our first sightseeing visit on our own, was a tour around the Pima Air & Space Museum. The volunteer tour guide knew his stuff and was obviously passionate about all things mechanical and flying. I had my own tour guide with me as it turns out that Mike's a plane geek; the model aeroplanes Mike built as a lad were here in life size. To say I was impressed was an understatement; a man of many talents, my hubby.

Us Scots are known for being thrifty; we like getting value for money, so when we heard about a discount book costing $20 which would save us quite a bit over the next few days in Tucson, it was a done deal.

You know the phrase, *lost in translation?* When we were buying our tickets, the receptionist suggested that we should try the *snoring dogs* in the cafe. I replied that I had a snoring dog at home and a snoring husband. It turned out that she was talking about a *Sonoran hot dog*, a local favourite. The lady's expression said it all, she thought I was bonkers!

Being tourists and armed with our discount book, *Book of Fun*, we visited the *Desert Museum* with its hummingbirds, mountain lions, wolves and so much more.

Then there was *Old Tucson;* had we just walked into a film set? Actually, yes we had. The old westerns were, and still are, filmed here. Film legends like John Wayne, the Duke, walked these dusty streets, or rather rode them.

Today, Old Tucson is where it's quite normal to see men throw themselves off rooftops after being 'shot' and there's folk laughing about it, including us!

As well as the stunt shows, the history of the Wild West comes alive in Old Tucson.

I wonder if the days of cowboys, gunslingers and stage-coaches were as violent as the old westerns made them out to be.

The next day, Kathy, Jim, and Carol (Kathy's sister) took us to Boot Hill Cemetery, Tombstone and the small quaint, arty town of Bisbee. I was gobsmacked; Tombstone isn't fictional after all, it's a real place with real history!

I wish, now, that I had paid more attention to the old westerns. I wasn't a fan of them really, preferring Star Trek instead!

- Here lies George Johnson, hanged by mistake 1882.
He was right ,we was wrong. But we strung him up and now he's gone'

The above epitaph is etched on a gravestone in Boothill Cemetery. It intrigued me; who was George Johnson?

Turns out that George wasn't famous when he was alive; he was an everyday man who, unfortunately, bought a stolen horse by mistake. Despite his pleas of innocence, George was convicted and sentenced to death by hanging.

Only after his death, the townsfolk realised that he had been innocent after all. Ooops! George's gravestone used to read '*George Johnson. Hanged by mistake*', replaced now with the above epitaph poem.

Poor Kathy and Jim; they must have visited here so many times with friends and visitors, but they patiently watched us "*Ooooh*" and "*Ahhh*" at each grave, especially George Johnson's. The people buried here were real people and usually met a violent death with their boots still on; hence the name.

A short drive further on from Boot Hill Cemetery, we arrived at Tombstone; I was beside myself with excitement! A real Wild West town! I could hardly contain myself as a stagecoach went by. It's like stepping back in time; a time where you had to be tough to survive or you would end up in Boot Hill Cemetery. I'm sure that Kathy and Jim were amused but also happy that we were having such an amazing day in their country.

Before a re-enactment of the '*OK Corale*', we browsed around the shops which were tastefully in keeping with the historic town. I got to thinking that Americans must enjoy coming to places such as Tombstone where the centre of the town is the hub, the heart, with shops, restaurants, and bars. It's a pity that their cities are quite often sterile and uninspiring. Driving to a mall doesn't have the same appeal as taking a bus into town and walking around the shops, stopping for lunch to chat to friends. This is where European towns and cities excel.

Leaving Tombstone, we drove down into the town of Bisbee; a quaint little place with the feel of Monschau in Germany; a town we used to visit quite often. Bisbee, with its curious little shops and artists, very much feels like it hasn't changed much since the 50's and seems to be a magnet for creative people to call home.

Could this day get even better? It most certainly did; we headed for lunch in a lovely Mexican restaurant Kathy and Jim knew about. Following on from our experiences in Mexico, Mexican restaurant means margaritas! Kathy was the first to order one, so I felt obliged to keep her company!

After lunch, we strolled around the town; Bisbee is in a valley and a lot of the buildings are built into the hill. Jim pointed out a set of steep steps which he had, in the past, run up without stopping. Fuelled on by margaritas and Mexican food; I was going to take on the challenge. After all, I'm Scottish and used to climbing up the steps in Edinburgh by the Mound. Cheered on by my pals, and being filmed, I flew up the steps; reaching the top I wished I had opted to do this before lunch!

Tucson is so close to the Mexican border that there are often passport control checks. As we were driving up to one, Mike announced that he had left his passport back at the tent (again!). On this trip, I carry my passport at all times so I was alright. We all chatted about what we would do if they stopped us. Would we say that Mike was American? Could he even pull off an American accent? Would we just hand him over to the authorities and bail him out after a night in the cell? Being the honest folk we are, we decided to come clean and say that he's left his passport and we would have to deal with the consequences, which probably meant, leave him behind!! We were stopped, but the soldier on duty didn't ask for ID; just looked through the window and wished us a nice day.

I just wonder if we had been a car of Hispanic people, would we have been asked for ID?

Reluctant to leave our new friends but knowing that we still had a long journey ahead of us, we jumped on our fully loaded bikes; said our goodbyes and left Tucson, vowing to return one day. Little did we know that Mike would be back sooner than we thought!

Our next big stop was the Grand Canyon but after leaving Tucson slightly later than planned, the ride would have to be done over two days. Our overnight stop was the mountain town of Payson; being just over three hours away from the

desert heat of Tucson, the cool, sweet mountain air of Payson was a welcome relief. Checking into a *Days Inn* meant that we could do some washing, have a proper bed, watch some TV and generally live it up for the night. Unfortunately every time we had a chance to watch TV, it was all about
the upcoming American Elections. Each time Donald Trump opens his mouth, and that's a lot, it's all over the news. Rather than subjecting ourselves to Trump, we left the sterile hotel room and ventured out.

Hearing country music coming from inside a bar, it sounded like the place to be. Opening the door and walking in, we were pleasantly surprised to find out that it was live music. This would do nicely.

Ever wanted to own a semi automatic AR 15 Assault Rifle? An unbelievable poster was pinned on the wall in the bar; just buy a ticket in the *Rim County Mule Deer Raffle* and you could be the proud owner of the rifle! I'm not sure what the postage to the UK would be, but I suspect it would start at about 10 years in jail!

Ever since our youngest, Hazel, had been attacked, Mike and I had been in almost daily contact with her wherever we managed to get internet access. The terrible feeling of helplessness followed us wherever we went; it was there each morning we woke up and still there as we dozed off at night.

Hazel was adamant that she didn't want us to go home and, after chatting to Kathy and our son, Daryl, we thought that we should respect how she felt and that, us going home, could make it worse. Where did I really want to be? Home looking after my little girl; I felt torn.

After video chatting Hazel in Payson, we knew then, that Hazel was far from OK. "*I'm going home Mike,*" I said.

"*I know; she needs her mum,*" he replied.

Then we contacted Kathy and Jim to ask if Mike could stay with them for a week; yet again we were overwhelmed by the generosity and kindness of people we had only just met. In fact, we hadn't even met Dale and his wife, Evelyn yet.

Before heading to Phoenix, we stayed another night in Payson frantically booking flights, arranging with Dale and Evelyn, Kathy and Jim.

Telling Hazel that I was heading home was emotional. She was furious but, I knew, relieved and so was I. I wanted to be with my little girl.

With our plans changed, we headed away from Payson back south towards Phoenix.

My flight was in the evening which gave us plenty of time to head straight to Dale and Evelyn's house outside Phoenix. We were getting used to the wide empty roads, so when we came up against the Phoenix drivers and congested roads, we were on our guard against idiot drivers. *What the hell?* How can I describe driving in Phoenix? Crazy! Choose a lane; it doesn't matter if it's the wrong one; just stay in it! Also using mobile phones, whilst driving, seems to be a normal thing to do over here.

Breathing a sigh of relief, we arrived at Dale and Evelyn's. Evelyn, Dale's wife, greeted us warmly as if we were old friends, "*come in, come in,*" she said, smiling.

Dale arrived home from work and drove me to the airport for the flight home via Heathrow. Mike stayed the night with Dale and Evelyn, joining them for a dinner night with friends before heading to Tucson and to Kathy and Jim's the following morning.

Finally home and wrapping my arms around my little girl, wanting to protect her; this was real life. This is what I'm all about; a mum, a wife and a grandmother. I'm here to protect my family, and, by jings, that's what I try to do. My little girl isn't a baby anymore; she's all grown up, a beautiful young woman.

But, she's still my little girl as my sons are my little boys; no matter how old they are.

Walking to the local shop that evening, arm in arm, Hazel told me what really happened that awful night; I felt numb.

Thinking back to that moment when Hazel told me; I feel

tears welling up. But, I'm in a public library writing this; I can't let the elderly man reading his book beside me see how I truly feel.

I think, not of what happened, but of my daughter, my brave, beautiful and strong daughter. To say that I'm in awe of Hazel, is an understatement. I have ornaments at home which depict our family; the ornament of Hazel is an angel. Hazel's not an angel and I jokingly tell people that the wings are stuck on with blue tack; which they really are! However, my daughter is an amazing young lady with the kindest heart and a fire burning in her which no man will extinguish.

The week went by too quickly and looming, was the flight back to the States; I didn't want to leave Hazel; I wanted to stay put and be there for her. For reasons I can't go into, I had to take that flight.

Cuddling up to Hazel in bed that morning before leaving, I sobbed.

"You're so brave Hazel," I cried,

"I'm not, I'm really not," she whispered in the darkness of the room.

There were mixed feelings landing back in Phoenix, but there was Mike standing waiting to wrap his arms around me. Seeing the pained expression on my face; he knew. My strong husband sobbed for his little girl; my turn to comfort Mike.

Dale sensed something was wrong and there was a respectful silence driving back to their house. Evelyn hugged me, handing me a much needed glass of wine. The table was set with a delicious meal which Evelyn had prepared for us. Jet lagged and emotionally drained, eating was the last thing on my mind; my body craved sleep.

The warmth of the light filtering through the curtains roused me from a surprisingly peaceful slumber. Then, realisation hit me.

Hazel! How was she? Should I suggest to Mike that we call off the trip and go back home? How would Hazel take the news, would she be angry?

Feeling overwhelmed, I took a deep breath and got dressed.

Saying our goodbyes to Evelyn and Dale, we thanked them for their kindness and hospitality; I know we'll see these lovely folk again.

Mike & Lynn's Big Trip:

Lynn arrived back in Phoenix, Arizona around 8pm last night. We are currently back in Payson, in the same hotel we left eight days ago and will be continuing Lynn & Mikes' Big Trip to the Grand Canyon tomorrow. I would like to thank all the good people, on both sides of the Atlantic, some of whom we have never even met, who offered assistance, support, accommodation, lifts and just general good wishes. Your kindness and willingness to go the extra mile in times of trouble has been truly humbling. Special thanks go to Kathy and Jim Weir, from Tucson who put me up at short notice for a week while Lynn was in the UK; and to Dale and Evelyn Doucet and the incredible organisation that is the Blue Knights for the hospitality, trips to the airport, a bed in Phoenix, food and friendship. I don't know what we would have done without you. We are in your debt and it will not be forgotten.

- Mike

Is this Groundhog Day? Here we were back in Payson, same hotel, same parking bays and, incredibly, the same receptionist as a week ago. Ditching our gear in the room, we headed out for a meal and a heart to heart. No live music this time. Instead, a lot of tears and a couple of bad margaritas!

We found ourselves standing on *the* corner with a lot of other people who were also wanting to stand on *the* corner! The band, the Eagles, put Winslow, Arizona on the map with their 1972 hit song, *'Take it Easy'*. This must be the most photographed corner in the world.

Although not a massive Eagles fan, I can't help but like this song. I wondered how much the local townsfolk like the song as it blares out repeatedly from the souvenir shop opposite the corner. I didn't know all of the words, but I do now!

Winslow isn't just about a corner; the town also sits in Navajo country in central-eastern Arizona. Winslow is home to 9,655 friendly people, according to the official city of Winslow website. The iconic Route 66 (US 66) runs through Main Street, the main highway until the I-40 (Interstate) bypassed Winslow.

Winslow. Without a doubt, the biggest attraction in Winslow is the corner. Many businesses and towns suffered when Route 66 was bypassed and this would have happened to Winslow if it hadn't been for the Eagles.

Just minutes from the I-40 and 26 miles from Winslow, is Meteor Crater. An asteroid travelling at 26,000 miles per hour colliding into the Earth 50,000 years ago, left a big hole; a really big hole! The crater stretches nearly a mile across and over 500 feet deep; that's a serious dent.

Mike, as usual, had done his research and knew that the RV park we were camping at was right by a section of the old Route 66. This section of the historic route is on private land and accessible by foot only. Changing from bike kit into our walking clothes, we took a hike back in time.

Walking in the heat along the now crumbling and dusty road, I tried to imagine Route 66 as it was in its heyday. The

Corvette Stingrays and the Chevy Bel Aires cruising America's Mother Road. Excited families going on vacation in their polished aluminium Airstreams. I wondered if I should feel sad because I didn't; it's just a road after all and the romance will always be there written in songs and books.

And the good news is that 85 percent of Route 66 is still driveable.

The old
Route 66

The sunsets whenever we have camped, have been incredible and the one we watched from the RV Park was turning the land a deep red. I still found it amazing to wake up, each morning in Arizona, knowing that the sun will most likely be shining uninterrupted in the sky.

Kathy told me that if clouds appear in the skies above Arizona, people celebrate by taking a day off work to enjoy the cool air. Complete opposite in Scotland, but for every drop of rain in Scotland, and we have a lot, is another drop of whisky (uisge beatha). Us Scots like to moan about the weather which, if you've ever visited Scotland in the summer, you'll understand why. So when the whole of June has been a *pish-oot,* we have to look on the bright side; mair (more) whisky!

After a night camped by the old Route 66, we loaded the

bikes and headed to Meteor Crater. Although a tourist attraction, the crater is still privately owned by the Barringer family and so is also known as Barringer Crater.

"It's just a big hole, that's all," we were told.

I suppose it depends on what floats your boat; we found the crater fascinating. Opting for the tour around the rim was a good decision as the guide delivered a riveting and animated talk about the crater, the meteorite that collided with the surface, the science and the Barringer family.

Lynn Aitken

**Meteor
Crater**

IF I COULD SOAR

The northwest corner of Arizona is home to the Grand Canyon. Here's the scientific stuff: 277 miles long, up to 18 miles wide and a mile deep carved out over millions of years by the mighty Colorado River.

You know when you have a picture in your head about what a place may be like and then you see it and it's not how you imagined it to be? Well, whenever I thought of the Canyon, I imagined a warm place and it is; but we were early in the season and at roughly 7,000 feet, I could feel the chill in the air. Only the South Rim was open; the North Rim being that much higher, was still closed and tourist free under a blanket of snow. Thank goodness for our fire pit; one of my fondest memories of the trip is sitting by the campfire chatting with a glass of wine or another wee tipple but I'll tell you about that later!

Kathy and Jim had packed up their RV and headed to the Canyon to spend a few days with us. They were staying in another part of the park, about 15 minutes walk through the trees from our site.

I love camping but it was nice to pop into the RV (recreational vehicle) for a cup of coffee, warm up, a blether and a proper seat.

The love affair that Americans have with their RVs is completely different to us in Europe. Just thinking about which motor home we would more likely see in the UK and straight away I visualize caravans being pulled by the family car. As soon as the holidays start, the caravans are packed up and heading towards the continent or exploring the UK.

The first time I saw an RV in the USA, I was flabbergasted at the sheer size of it. It was the size of a single-decker bus and pulling a car! I was even more amazed when I saw the side being extended by the driver pushing a button; a slide out, I think they call it. This makes the RV even larger! These RVs are bigger than some of the houses in the UK!! Kathy and Jim's RV wasn't as big as this and Kathy said that people called their RV *quaint*. In the UK, however, Kathy and Jim's RV would be considered large and there would be quite a few of our twisty roads in Scotland that wouldn't be suitable for it.

Meeting up with our good friends in the park shop, there were hugs all round. Kathy was so excited about showing us the Grand Canyon that she suggested that we take the shuttle bus straight away to the rim. Another great service in a lot of the national parks, is the shuttle bus. It means that you can leave the car, or in our case, motorbikes and enjoy the scenery while someone else does the driving as well as keeping the roads uncongested and less pollution.....win win.

Walking the short distance from getting off the bus to the rim, we were about to get our first sight of the Grand Canyon. I could feel myself holding my breath as we drew closer. I wanted to be overwhelmed, amazed, bowled over, speechless and in awe. Although I knew that this was going to be one of the most amazing sights I had ever seen; nothing could have prepared me for the immensity of the Canyon. And the colours of the different layers of rock, telling a story of how our planet was formed. How can I describe the Grand Canyon? The immense vastness is breathtakingly beautiful and really beyond describing. Photos don't do this natural wonder justice. All I can suggest is that, if you ever get the chance to visit the Canyon, please go and witness the Grand Canyon for yourself.

Over the next four days, we explored the Canyon with Kathy and Jim. Kathy constantly surprised me with her knowledge and passion for the history of the Native Americans and Mary Colter. Who's Mary Colter? Mary Jane Elizabeth Colter was the chief architect and decorator for the Fred Harvey

Company from 1902 to 1948, and who designed many of the buildings in the Grand Canyon; one of them being the Desert View Watchtower. Perched at Desert View, standing sentry over the Grand Canyon, the Watchtower seems to 'grow' from the land itself. That was Mary Colter's vision; it's clear that she took inspiration from the surrounding landscape.

Upstairs in the Watchtower looking over the Grand Canyon, is the Hopi Room which is decorated with paintings by Hopi artist, Fred Kabotie. The largest mural on the wall, being the story of the first Hopi person to travel down the Colorado River. We were lucky to be at the Watchtower just in time to listen to Ed Kabotie, Fred's grandson. Born on a day when there were snow clouds above the surrounding mountains, Ed was named 'Okhuwa P'ing' meaning Cloud Mountain; his Native name.

Singing in his native tongue, Ed sang songs and told us stories, in English, which all expressed the values of his Native American culture. The passion Ed has for his history and culture was infectious; I could have listened to him all day.

The relationship, stretching over eons, between the Canyon and the tribes was and still is crucial. It was sad, also, to hear of how the natural resources are being exploited and taken away from these proud people to feed an unnatural city like Las Vegas. We were heading there soon and planning to spend a couple of days in Sin City. This was a place on our trip that didn't appeal to me however, Las Vegas is also on the way to Death Valley. I also felt that I would like to see the city in the desert for myself and make my own mind up about it. Our niece, Nicolle and our sister-in-law, Jean, both love Las Vegas.

"There's something for everyone in Las Vegas," Jean told us.

But, with Ed Kabotie's words resonating in my head, I wasn't so sure. The days spent with Kathy and Jim exploring the Grand Canyon were incredible; spending time with our friends and being privileged to experience this unique and wondrous place on our planet. At each viewpoint, we were awestruck again and again.

"*No more snow at Grand Canyon*," the Park Information Office said.

"*OK, maybe a few flurries*," they said.

"*OK, but it won't lie*," they said.

"*Oh really?*" Mike said.

Sitting in the El Tovar restaurant on our last evening at the Canyon, the four of us looked out at the blizzard blowing past the windows. Now thoughts were turning to wondering if we would be able to leave tomorrow. But, more important and pressing, was our tent still standing?

Walking out of the restaurant, the cold air hit us, stinging our faces. At least it had stopped snowing and the wind had died down; the storm now passed, the sky was clear and I looked up at the stars.

Saying goodnight to Kathy and Jim, we crunched through the snow back to our tent. What a lovely sight; the tent was still standing, albeit bowing under the weight of a covering of snow. Carefully we brushed most of the soft powdery snow off the tent before climbing into our sleeping bags. With a few layers of clothes on, and the fluffy blanket Kathy lent us; we hoped to stay warm.

"*Yer aff yer heid*!" would have been my answer to Mike's suggestion to go camping in the middle of the winter. For non-Scottish readers, this translates as, "*You're off your head*."

At no point did we feel cold that last night in our cosy wee tent in the Grand Canyon. We found that keeping our day clothes inside our sleeping bags at the bottom means that they're nice and warm to change into.

An ice-kissed winter wonderland greeted us in the morning. It was still below zero and there was no way we could ride our bikes until the temperature rose. Trudging back through the snow, we knew that Kathy would greet us with a hot, strong *wake me up* coffee.

And sure enough, two strong, hot coffees were handed to us as we stepped into the warmth of the RV.

After a last blether, it was time to say cheerio to Kathy and Jim but we know we'll meet up again, either in Scotland or back in the US.

By the time we packed up the tent and loaded the bikes, some of the snow had melted. Still bitterly cold, at least the roads looked clear of snow. Hopefully, this was as cold as it was going to get; at 7000 feet, we were heading downhill so we would be riding into warmer temperatures.

Following Mike, we headed away from the Grand Canyon, vowing to return one day. The roads were mostly clear but soon realised that, in sheltered places, there were treacherous patches of ice. Seeing Mike up ahead skid slightly, I knew we would have to take it easy. Maybe we should have stayed a day or so longer in the Canyon, but the weather could have gotten a whole lot worse.

I'm not just a fair weather rider and, although it's nice to ride when the sun is shining and the air is warm, riding in the rain and wind doesn't bother me. Ice, though, is a whole different ball game. Through choice; no, I wouldn't ride in icy conditions and we had underestimated how bad it actually was, but we were committed now. Slow, steady and avoiding dodgy parts of the road; we forged ahead. A few small slides but we made it and soon, due to us leaving the lofty heights of the South Rim, the air was warming up and so were we. I even switched off my heated grips. Heated grips? I hear you say! Yes, I'm on an adventure but it's nice to have some luxuries.

Not long after leaving the winter wonderland of Grand Canyon, we were soon stripping off some layers as the temperatures rose. Where to next? Zion National Park in Utah. But rather than whizz there in half a day, we were stopping to see Horseshoe Bend on the outskirts of the town of Page.

The spectacular curve in the Horseshoe Bend, Arizona, is one of the most photographed places in the world and you can see why.

Directly off Highway 89 we found the trail head leading to the Bend which is a 1.5-mile round-trip hike. In cooler clothes rather than bike kit, the walk would have been a nice stretch of the legs. The sand under foot, or rather boot, made it tough going and we were soon dripping in sweat.

There was a steady line of people heading there and another returning. Looking down from above, we must have looked like two lines of ants. Instead of carrying food, the line retracing their steps back from the Bend were carrying memories and photos.

The 270° Horseshoe Bend in the Colorado River is known as an incised meander; that's what I read when researching this magical place. I don't understand geology but gazing down at the Horseshoe Bend with no guardrails, I was in awe. Wouldn't it be amazing if a time lapse camera could have captured the Earth's formation and compressed millions of years into a couple of hours? That would be incredible. Or would it just blow our minds?

"No more snow," they said!

ZION NATIONAL PARK; UTAH

After the Horseshoe Bend and staying a night in the small town of Page, we headed on towards Zion National Park. I feel guilty when I don't write much about a town such as Page, but we're travelling through so many places which makes it nigh on impossible to see everything on the way through. Looking out of the hotel window, I could see the glistening waters of Lake Powell. A walk to explore Page and walk around the shores of Lake Powell was tempting, but it was late and I was tired and turning away from the window, the hotel bed was looking inviting.

The next morning, we left Arizona and entered the state of Utah. An interesting name so I had to find out what it meant. *Utah* comes from the name of the Ute Native American tribe, meaning *people of the mountains*

So, what else is Utah famous for? Green Jell-O Salad, it's not your usual salad, this one wobbles! Utahans don't just eat Jell-O; they happily slide in it and sculpt with it. Jell-O, to us Brits, is Jelly, by the way.

On a serious note, Utah is also home to Zion National Park. This breathtakingly beautiful wilderness has it all; sandstone canyons, deserts, plateaus, waterfalls and the waters of the Virgin River flowing through.

Zion National Park has three entrances, depending on which direction you come from.

From Page, we arrived at the East Entrance which meant we would be riding through the 1.1 miles long Zion-Mount Carmel Tunnel.

What a spectacular entrance into the park. It was also our very first sighting of American buffalo. I have only ever seen these magnificently proud beasts on Westerns when they roamed the grasslands and were hunted to near-extinction by the U.S. Cavalry. The native Americans respected the buffalo and only hunted them for survival; every part of the animal was used, nothing wasted, as it should be. So, to see these beasts grazing was, for us, a memory we will always treasure. The good news is that the numbers of buffalo are steadily increasing.

Riding out of the tunnel and back into daylight; we were in spectacular scenery. Had we stumbled into a land that time forgot? It certainly looked that way. I can't say which national park is the most beautiful as they are all stunning and yet so different from each other. Grand Canyon is vast, unbelievable and you can see for miles; in Zion, most of the time, we were looking up at the canyon walls towering above us.

We were directed to the Watchman Campsite by the South Entrance of the park. Named after the rocky peak which rises above the site; our tent/home, was pitched in a most stunning location. Grand Canyon wasn't that far away from Zion really, but temperature wise, Zion and Grand Canyon were in two different seasons. Gone was the icy chill of Grand Canyon, replaced with Zion basking in summer heat. Here, in Zion, the tent would have time to dry out after the snows.

The campsite is a short walk to the small and charming town of Springdale which sits just outside the entrance to the park. The permanent population of 500 welcomes a couple of million visitors each year to the picturesque town. I loved the atmosphere here; the little curio shops, the happy people strolling leisurely and then there was the ice cream parlour!

Sitting enjoying a coffee (I had already finished my ice cream!), we watched a group of prisoners sweeping the street supervised by a Police Officer. I immediately heard Sam Cooke's lyrics, *Chain Gang*, in my head. This was a chain gang without the chains. How did I know that they were prisoners? They had *PRISONER* printed on their sweatshirts. Community service, we would call it in the UK, but I have never seen it, not like this. Why aren't the British prisoners serving time, out there, in the streets, cleaning up? That would stop them getting bored, good exercise and helping their communities. Human rights, I guess!

Zion, although stunningly beautiful, is not a destination for everyone. The visitor to Zion is someone who loves the outdoors and being at one with nature. Our camping neighbour rose each morning and headed down to the river; yoga mat rolled up under her arm for her meditation, whilst photographers set up their cameras to capture the rising sun over the rocky peaks. All like-minded people, enjoying the beauty and serenity of Zion.

And yet, in this beautiful place, my heart went out to Mike. Being an active man all his life and still is, Mike's knackered knees limit him to how much walking he can do. There was a time when we would have scrambled up to the heady heights of Angel's Landing. Being in Zion was a bit like having a box of chocolates and being told that you could look, smell but only imagine how it would taste.

Being the determined and proud man he is, Mike managed a couple of the gentler hikes which were stunning and the pain afterwards was worth it....Mike's words! When he gets his new knees, we'll bag some Munros and maybe even go back to Zion to climb Angel's Landing. Or, even better, hike down to the bottom of the Grand Canyon and climb up the next day;

now that's on our bucket list.

BEAUTY TO BEDLAM

Glancing in my wing mirror, I saw the jagged peaks of Zion getting smaller as we rode further away. Leaving such a beautiful place is always a bit sad; but so much more to discover and we're really fortunate to have the opportunity to go on this adventure of a lifetime.

We were back on the open road and before we knew it, we had crossed from Utah into Nevada; the *Silver State.*

I had heard about the gold rush but knew nothing of the silver rush, which happened roughly the same time as the gold rush. Often lying on the surface of the ground, silver was easier and quicker to find and extract. Small boomtowns appeared wherever silver was discovered, but once it was depleted, the towns were abandoned. Still, to this day, there are remnants of the silver rush days; the ghost towns of Nevada.

There is nothing ghostly about our Nevada destination; situated in a basin on the floor of the Mojave Desert, Las Vegas is a mere 160 miles from Zion National Park and yet, it could have been a 1000 miles. The two landscapes are worlds apart. Finding ourselves in a dusty basin with mountains all around, we rode towards Sin City.

Out of nowhere, wallop! We were blasted side on by a hot, dry crosswind. The closer we got to Vegas, the stronger the wind. Thank goodness we didn't have intercoms because Mike would've heard "*Aaaaaah! Aaaaaah! Shit! Aaaaaaah!*" That was me! I was holding on for dear life, hoping not to be blown across the highway. Looking ahead at Mike, I could see him being knocked sideways so readied myself for the same blast of wind. It was so exhausting that we had to take a break at a gas station before taking on the wind once again. Getting off our bikes, we both looked at each other and shook our heads. That was tough and my arm muscles were shaking from keeping my bike upright and going straight ahead.

Muscles loosened, we jumped on the bikes continuing towards the desert city. We could see Vegas a way ahead of us for what seemed like a long time. Being daylight, Vegas didn't look like Vegas, if you see what I mean.

Arriving on the outskirts of the city and it still didn't look like the Las Vegas I had seen on photos. On either side of the road and on street corners, there were shanty towns with impoverished looking people hanging around; clearly stoned.

The overpowering smell of weed hung like a cloud over this part of Vegas; cloying and sickly. *Can you get high on third hand weed?* I was wondering.

This wasn't the Las Vegas I had imagined; where were the bright lights, the glitz and glamour? *Do the millions of tourists flying into Vegas ever see this?*

Las Vegas is a city of contrast; hunger and poverty to an abundance of everything. I'm glad that we're seeing the real places that we're riding through with people living real lives; again, I'm thankful that we have the National Health Service in the UK. We have homelessness, but not like we have seen in the USA. Saying I'm glad about seeing poverty isn't the correct way of putting it; I would rather see everything rosy and people happy and healthy, but that's not the way of the world, I'm afraid.

Tourists who go on holiday to the resorts, stay where it's safe and fly home again with a glowing tan, aren't seeing the real country.

Ahead, leaving the shanty towns behind, was downtown Las Vegas. Towering above the city, was a tall, golden glass building with 'TRUMP' emblazoned on the top. That should have been an omen warning me about this place!

We weren't going to camp in Vegas but we certainly weren't going to be staying in Trump Hotel! Even if we could have afforded it, throwing money away to line Trump's pockets would never be an option.

So, a nice cheap and cheerful hotel for us.

It was easier than I had thought it would be, riding into Vegas, finding the hotel and parking. You know how I said that the hotel was cheap and cheerful? Cheap (ish), yes, cheerful, most definitely not. The receptionist glowered at us through her 'over the top' false eyelashes.

"*Yes?*" she asked, obviously wishing that we weren't there.

"*Hi, we've got a reservation,*" I announced cheerfully, whilst actually thinking, *Oh, I'm sorry I'm annoying you by asking you to do your job.*

Welcome to Vegas, I thought. There was an invisible tension brewing and Mike knew that I was *simmering*. She was the first rude person we met on the trip; I wasn't going to let this bad-mannered individual ruin our day, so, reluctantly, I kept my mouth shut.

Daylight was fading, giving way to the famous neon lights of Sin City; Las Vegas now looked exactly how I imagined it would. Venturing out, we headed for the Strip, which is actually south of Las Vegas city limits. People we have chatted to prior to the trip who love the Las Vegas experience, recommended Fremont Street. That would be our second night in Vegas. Tonight we would explore, soak up the atmosphere and go for a meal. Wandering around dodging drunk people, ticket selling touts and Elvis (I'm joking about Elvis!), it was a surreal experience. I was really trying to enjoy the city and all it has to offer but I just couldn't. When I saw a glitzy, tacky version of the Eiffel Tower, I knew that this place wasn't for me.

Taking Mike's arm, I whispered, "*Mike, I don't want to seem ungrateful, but I hate it here.*"

Mike gently squeezed my arm, "*me too,*" he replied.

We couldn't leave Vegas without going into Caesar's Palace. Quintessentially Las Vegas, it just has to be done. This was bling in overdrive! Tourists, us included, walked around looking overwhelmed and blown away. As large and spacious as Caesar's Palace is, I felt claustrophobic; my instinct was to turn around and leave.

The noise, the rows upon rows of slot machines, the hopeful feeding the machines with coins, free drinks flowing as long as the machines are being fed.

Sitting with their free drinks, smoking cigarettes, the ethereal light from the machines, reflecting in the gamblers' staring eyes.

These people are on holiday, they should look happy, I thought. Instead, they looked miserable, fixated and almost angry. Oh for the natural beauty of the Grand Canyon or Zion.

"Let's go for a drink before dinner," Mike suggested. *"at least we can say that we've had a drink in Caesar's Palace"* he added.

"$9 for a bottle of Coors!"

"There's no way I'm paying $9 for a bottle of Coors!"

"Can you believe that? $9 for a bottle of Coors!" Mike repeated in a state of shock.

"That's it, let's get the fork out of here" he added.

"I think we should find somewhere for dinner," I suggested.

Stepping back out into the heat, we looked up at the sky. It was like the 1984 film *Ghostbusters*; the final scenes with the woman (played by Sigourney Weaver) on the rooftop of her apartment. The night sky, churning, boiling and angry; a vortex was going to suck the City of Lights off the face of the Earth.

Looking up at the eerie sky, a tiny, lone helicopter was flying over the city. *It's like the end of the world,* I thought.

Sitting in an Italian restaurant away from the madness of the city, we felt like we had just run the gauntlet.

"Do you want to stay another night?" I asked Mike.

"Absolutely not!" he replied, shaking his head. Obviously still in shock over the $9 Coors! *"What about leaving tomorrow?"* Mike suggested.

Decision made, we were leaving in the morning; Las Vegas wasn't for us.

The next morning, our breakfast in Las Vegas confirmed the reason we were leaving that day. Looking for the breakfast room, we eventually found it after walking through smoky gambling halls filled with dazed people who appeared to have been there all night. Breakfast consisted of everything wrapped in plastic, with coffee in plastic cups and flimsy plastic plates using plastic cutlery.

Sorry Las Vegas, but we won't be back, like ever!

With Las Vegas far behind us, we left Nevada. We were really 'bagging' the States. This time, the Golden State of California and home to Death Valley. Known as the hottest, lowest and driest National Park; with places such as Furnace Creek and Badwater Basin, why would anyone contemplate going here? It's a fascinating wilderness, that's why.

The wilderness, though, was teeming with people. It was the most crowded 'middle of nowhere' I had ever seen. And the reason for this was the Super Bloom. This rare event happens only if the conditions are perfect and the recent El Nino has provided that. Seeds dormant for years, spring to life turning this unforgiving land into a valley of colour.

Looking back, we should have felt privileged to be in Death Valley at this momentous time, but coming from a land of greenery and lots of colour, we are used to this. Tiny yellow wildflowers carpeted the land on either side of the road and amongst the flowers, people meditating, taking photos and couples walking hand in hand. This truly was a rare phenomenon and the fact that we weren't expecting this; what an honour.

People had flocked to Death Valley from far afield, resulting in 'no room at the inn'. We wanted to camp, but no spaces, not even for our wee tent. Well, that wasn't entirely true; there was a small space for our tent, but after the night in Big Bend, we now looked more carefully at the area before setting up camp.

The only place available in Death Valley had the potential for another *Big Bend* experience. Open, desert, surrounding hills and hot, extremely hot; a recipe for disaster.

"Ok," I decided, *"let's get a hotel room"*

We asked at the Visitor Centre but there was nothing unless we had booked, which of course, we hadn't. We hadn't planned on the Super Bloom.

The daylight would be fading soon so we had to get a move on and out of Death Valley if we wanted to try and find somewhere to stay the night. The ride that dusk was truly magnificent. Stopping briefly to have a look at the map (we found maps more accurate than Sat Nav), we watched in awe as the sun set on Death Valley. Looking down on this magical place, I wondered about the name, Death Valley. Watching the land and mountains turn shades of red, orange and gold, it is so beautiful and at the same time, as the name hints, harsh and deadly.

The fiery colours quickly faded, replaced by the velvet blanket of night. With the sun gone for the night, thoughts returned to finding somewhere to sleep. The desert heat had disappeared to be replaced by a cold which seeped right through us. Even with the extra layers and our heated grips on max, I was starting to shiver. We rode for nearly two hours until finally arriving in a small town called Lone Pine. It reminded me of a song but I was too cold to sing! Yes! A room! We were going to sleep well in Lone Pine.

In the morning, I woke early enough to go for a walk. Heading out of the hotel, I stopped in my tracks and stared up in amazement! Arriving in the dark, we hadn't seen the beautiful, snowy Mount Whitney towering over the town. From the heat of Death Valley, Mount Whitney remained suspended in winter.

Whenever we're packing our bikes, we usually attract an audience, and in Lone Pine, this was no exception. A man who had just checked out of the hotel wandered over to ask where we were from, where we were heading to; the usual questions.

"You're never going to get all of that onto those two bikes', he challenged us, smiling.

"Oh really?" I thought.

Suitably impressed, the man handed us two $2 bills. My baffled look was answered. *"That's for luck,"* he said, *"they're quite rare and I would like to give them to you. Keep them with you on your journey."*

Feeling humbled, we thanked the kind gentleman and said our goodbyes. The $2 bills have stayed with us and I'm planning on framing them as a little reminder of the kindness of the people we've met along the way.

Leaving Lone Pine, I wondered why Mike was passing the junction we were meant to take. I followed on behind, expecting him to make a U-Turn and head back, shaking his head as he usually does. But, no; he kept going.

A few miles further on, he signalled to the right, riding into a lay by with a small building.

There'll be a reason, I thought.

Smiling, Mike took me by the hand and led me over to the stone plaque with the name of the town etched on it.

'Armistead'

My maiden name!! Mike had obviously noticed this when he was planning the route. It's such an unusual name that I hardly ever hear of it, let alone a town called Armistead! I wanted to know why, how the town got its name. When I say 'town', I actually mean a couple of buildings, one of which was the store/museum where we had parked. Surely the folk in the store would be able to tell us the story behind the name; but, unfortunately not. The young lass behind the counter looked uninterested and clearly didn't know.

SEQUOIA; A LAND OF GIANTS

Sequoia National Park, as the name hints, is home to the giant Sequoia trees and the daddy of them all, *General Sherman*; the largest living tree on the planet.

These magnificent trees grow naturally in just one place, the Sierra Nevada mountain range at an elevation of between 5,000 and 8,000 feet.

Entering into a world of greenery and trees, I was excited beyond belief. Living in Perthshire with ancient forests on our doorstep, I feel at home amongst the trees walking the dog. Scroggiehill Woods were our children's playground; summers meant picnics, den-building, making bows and arrows and exploring. From a young lad making bows and arrows in Scroggiehill, Vaughan, our oldest son, still ventures up there at 31 years old to find the right branch for making his bows; a passion he still has.

We chose our campsite and pitched the tent, aware of this being bear country, so all food and toiletries were stored away in the bear boxes which each site has. If there wasn't a bear box, we tended to store the food in our top boxes but most National Park campsites provide the boxes.

This was truly idyllic. A herd of mule deer wandered quite happily by, munching on grass and inquisitive ground squirrels popped their heads out of their holes before bounding out looking for food.

The animals are protected in the parks which is great, but

I guess if these deer step outside the boundaries, then it's venison for a local hunter. The next morning we headed up to the lofty heights of the park where the Sequoias live. Riding up the stunning twisty road, the greenery was soon replaced by snow and ice; the trees were getting larger. Elevation of over 7000 feet, it was darn cold. The youngster in me was thinking *Yippee! Snow!* And the older part of me, *by jings, it's cold!*

Parking the bikes, we trudged through the snow over to (what we thought) General Sherman. Seeing the small group of people by the tree, posing, taking photos; I was thinking, *It's impressive, I admit, but there's one over yonder much more impressive.*

Realising that we were all at the wrong tree, as remarkable as it was, we wandered over to the real General Sherman.

From afar and even more so, up close, General Sherman was the most incredible tree I had ever seen. Craning my neck to look up and amazed at the width, I felt privileged, humbled, tiny and in awe at this most wondrous tree.

The stories these ancient giants could tell us; but, would we listen? Riding back down the twisties, I felt energised, alive and I a lot warmer as we left the snow behind.

From our campsite, there was a sign-posted trail to Marble Falls. It was a fair hike but nice to get out of breath and stretch the legs. Mike's knees were having a good day and the walk wasn't too taxing; tomorrow could be a different matter altogether.

Could this day get any better? What a beautiful waterfall; the water cascading over sparkling, white rock.

"Wow Mike! The stone looks just like marble!"

Shaking his head and smiling, *"the clue's in the name hon!"*

I loved Sequoia National Park and was bemused to read a book recently about the best national parks in America, and Sequoia didn't even feature! I guess there are so many of them and maybe Sequoia isn't to everyone's taste; we were glad to have experienced the park and met General Sherman and his friends.

YOSEMITE NATIONAL PARK

Staying in California, we left Sequoia and headed to the bigger and better known, Yosemite. Compared to the tranquil Sequoia, visitors flock to Yosemite and certain areas of the park can be crowded during the peak season. Although we were going in March, the quieter time, we still thought it best to find a place to stay outside the park in the town of Oakhurst, 14 miles from Yosemite.

Dropping by Oakhurst Visitor Centre, they were kind enough to secure us a hotel room at a good price. Mike's Sat Nav wasn't working......sore point! But, he set off in search of the hotel, and me as his wingman, followed.

Wrong hotel! Half the name was correct; *Inn.* We thought about trying to find the right hotel but were greeted by such a cheerful lady at the front desk who offered us a room at a good rate; that we stayed put.

The receptionist was the most helpful we had met up till now; nothing was too much trouble. *Ms Las Vegas* could learn a thing or two!
Always smiling, the hotel clerk in Oakhurst, even did our washing for us, including my Sssssh.....bra. I washed my undies though. Is that too much information?

The 14 miles from Oakhurst to Yosemite was a scenic one, with curves and twisties and smells.

Without the confines of being in a car, senses are heightened; you notice every smell you pass; be it the citrusy aroma of pine trees, wild garlic or manure! The scents around us, the road, the sun warming my face; all intensified my excitement about visiting Yosemite.

Riding into the park, I saw the entrance to Wawona Tunnel up ahead. Raising my sun visor, I followed Mike through the mouth of the road tunnel, letting my eyes adjust to the orange glow from the lights above us.

After a mile riding through the coolness of Wawona, up ahead I could see the exit; now I know where the phrase, *the light at the end of the tunnel,* comes from. Like moths attracted to a lamp, we rode towards the light.

What a vista! We immediately parked to take in the view and what a view it was. The valley stretches out far below with the monumental granite El Capitan to the left, the Bridal Veil Falls, its waters cascading down over 600 ft and the curved Half Dome standing watch.

There's no need to describe these sights really, as the names are description enough. Take away all the tourists and the roads and this enchanting place could be a prehistoric scene from *The Land Before Time* with dinosaurs grazing down on the valley floor and pterodactyls flying in the skies above El Capitan.

Riding through Yosemite and stopping to view cascading waterfalls and alpine valleys. Although not overly crowded, I was still glad that we were staying back in Oakhurst and taking a day trip to Yosemite.

This is wine country and it would be disrespectful of us not to sample the local beverage. Cue, the *Idle Hour Winery* in Oakhurst! Idle Hour, I like that name. We were planning to have an excellent Idle Hour, or two!

This is where we met Jan and her colleague, Doug. Sampling the delicious Californian tipple, we enjoyed a blether with them. I know I keep saying this, but it's the people we're meeting along the way who are making this trip extra special. Jan and Doug, thank you for the great craic, and Jan, thank you

Lynn Aitken

so much for the bottles of wine.

SAN FRANCISCO

Leaving Oakhurst heading west, our next port of call was the city everyone loves, San Francisco. Well, that's what we've been told so we're about to find out.

The campsite on the outskirts of San Francisco could have been a supermarket car park, but without the store. Tesco and Sainsbury are missing a trick! Not only could they charge for camping there, they've got a captive audience who needs food, toilets and general everyday comforts! Let's not give them any ideas!

Being the only people with a tent, we had a lovely grassed area to ourselves, but the poor folk with RVs could hardly open their doors without bashing their neighbours. Opposite was a building site where the demolishing of the San Francisco 49ers Candlestick Park Stadium was taking place. Not the most idyllic setting I admit, but this is a city and we can't be choosy.

I walked around the car park, oops, I mean campsite trying to catch a glimpse of the Golden Gate Bridge, but no luck. I could hardly wait to get into the city and do the touristy bit and explore.

Apart from having the bikes serviced at the BMW dealer, we would be using the public transport as much as possible. And there's one mode of transport which is iconic to San

Francisco.....the cable car. *Ding, ding, ding* I've seen them in the films with people hanging onto the outside of the cars as they travel up and down the steep streets of the city.

Smiling from ear to ear, I hung onto the outside of the cable car as we climbed up and over Nob Hill (interesting name!) continuing down to Bay Street and the hustle and bustle of Fisherman's Wharf. Frisco was on my tick list and I was loving every minute of it.

Unfortunately, we hadn't booked in advance for a trip out to Alcatraz, the infamous Federal Penitentiary. Fully booked for the next month! Lesson learned, note to self; check and book in advance.

After collecting our bikes from the BMW dealer, we took a ride out to the top of Lombard Street, the *crookedest street* in the world. It was blawing a hoolie, (windy) and raining. Mike started down Lombard Street first and I followed a few seconds later. Every man and his dog come here to drive or ride down Lombard Street, so it's busy, really busy! On either side, I noticed tourists taking photographs of us daft people going down the street.

Oh shit, I thought, *if I fall off, I'm going to be an internet sensation!*

Do you know that people actually live on this street? I found that out, half way down, when a garage door opened and a car started reversing out in front of me. Bikes don't have a reverse gear so I had to stop (on an extremely steep, crooked street!) and wait on the car coming out of the garage before continuing down to the bottom of the street where Mike was waiting. And, before you go checking *You Tube* for a crazy lady biker on a red GS falling off on Lombard Street, you're wasting your time because I didn't. Phew!

Determined to cram as much as we could into our few days here, we took some time to explore Chinatown. Everyone we spoke to about San Francisco, said that we shouldn't miss this. San Francisco's Chinatown is the largest outside of Asia. What can I say that won't offend our family and friends who recommended Chinatown to us? It was OK and that's all I can say. Lots of plastic waving cats, too many tourists and weird looking fish in tanks that, in my opinion, were too small.

The historic Fisherman's Wharf, on the other hand, was a fun place to explore. Yes, it's a real tourist trap with souvenir shops, overpriced restaurants and crowds but I couldn't help but enjoy the craziness of the Wharf. From here, we hired a couple of bicycles and cycled over the famous Golden Gate Bridge which, by the way, looks like the Forth Road Bridge painted red. Cycling over the bridge was a logistical nightmare! People walking, countless bicycles and too many speeding, cantankerous road racers, all fighting for space.

Stopping for a photo shot on the return cycle, we watched a fisherman struggling with a bird, Shag, I think. Instead of a fish, the man had hooked the bird by accident.

He was now trying to free it but nobody had told the bird that and it was frenziedly pecking the man's hands. Mike ran over to help and between the two of them, the bird was freed, but not until it had taken a nip at Mike's hand. Diving back into the water, it shook itself and looked none the worst for its experience. Mike and the man looked happy with their effort and the obvious admiration of the on-looking crowd, me included. Both nursing their wounds, they said their goodbyes.

As long as I can remember, I've loved watching people and the best places for this pastime are in cities. It's nice to just sit, stop for a while and watch people living their lives. *Where are they going*? I wonder, *are they wondering what to cook for tea tonight*? Sitting in a cafe in San Francisco, we enjoyed a coffee and watching the world go by. Gazing out the window, we spotted a poor homeless man wearing a bin bag which didn't cover his bits & bobs! A policeman on a bicycle stopped and moved the man on, probably to another street corner, poor guy.

We were sitting at one of those communal tables in the cafe where strangers awkwardly sit beside each other and usually on their phones or laptops. Opposite was a regular guy sipping a coffee, headphones on and typing away on his laptop. Next to him sat another guy with a, *oh my giddy aunt, a knife!!* I don't mean a butter knife either. This was a switchblade. The guy with the knife caught me looking at him and, playfully, ran his fingers down the sharp side of the blade. Regular guy with headphones was oblivious.

How do I warn the normal guy? I wondered. Just then, he glanced across the table at me. *This is my chance*, I realised. From behind my hand, I mouthed silently, "*he's got a knife*," my eyes signalling to the weirdo.

The normal, regular guy looked somewhat confused but then glanced to his side, saw the knife and cottoned on to the fact that he was sitting next to a potential mass killer. Do you think I'm being over dramatic?
Weirdo realises that we were onto him and shuts his knife

away.

And that, was San Francisco.

The road leaving the quirky city that is San Francisco, took us over the Golden Gate Bridge and north on Highway 1. I noted, smiling, that the bridge was as crowded as the day we cycled over it.

Away from the city, buildings were soon replaced by fields, trees and the freedom of the road. I had a warm and fuzzy feeling knowing that we weren't the only ones heading north, up the Pacific Coast. The distinguished and magnificent gray whales we had seen off Baja, were now migrating back home to Alaska with their young. We didn't catch sight of them, but it was nice to know that they were there, just taking the watery road.

"You're going to love the ride along the Pacific Coast, the views are amazing," we were promised.

There are miles and miles of stunning coastline riding north from San Francisco, that is true. The road hugs the land, so one minute the ocean is there in full view and the next, hidden behind hills and shrubbery. However, we come from an island with some of the finest coastal scenery in the world, so we weren't blown away by the Pacific Coast.

Now that I've either upset our American buddies or promoted the British tourism industry, I'll move on.

Stopping for the night in the quaint little town of Bodega Bay was a must. Famous for Alfred Hitchcock's 1963 film; *The Birds* which was filmed in this charming fishing village and also, the San Andreas Fault which runs right through the middle of the bay. *The Birds* was fictional but the San Andreas Fault is very real, a time bomb below our feet.

Then there are the *Tsunami Evacuation Route* signposts which are dotted in various places throughout Bodega Bay. I felt like I was on a ship or a plane, I kept looking for the emergency exits! And that would be up; just climb up as fast as you can!

California is wine country, so a spot of wine tasting was

order of the day. Sitting on a balcony soaking up the warm evening sun, we sipped wine whilst gazing over the calm waters of the bay. At the next table, another couple were enjoying the view with a glass of wine. It wasn't long before we got chatting to our table neighbours. It turned out that the couple were frequent visitors to Bodega Bay.

"Did you know that the movie, 'The Birds' was filmed here?" the lady asked us.

"Yes, I do," I replied, *"it was so scary in its day. But, the Fault is more scary,"* I added

"Fault? What Fault?"

"You know, The San Andreas Fault? It runs right through the bay," I confirmed, wondering if she was 'having us on'

I realised, when she put her glass of wine down, that she was deadly serious.

"A fault? Here? You mean right here?" pointing at the calm waters of the bay.

"Er, yes. The San Andreas Fault."

Looking at her husband, she asked, *"Did you know that there's a fault running right through here?"*

Thinking back, I don't think her husband did know, but he nodded anyway, whilst looking at the water worryingly.

Oops, I thought, *new holiday destination perhaps?*

Mike and I held it together until we started walking back to the B&B, then we let rip. We laughed so much, partly due to the wine, but also the fact that she knew all about the film, *The Birds*, but not about the potentially imminent danger lurking beneath the ground.

Passing by a sweetie shop, I spotted something called *Salt Water Taffy* and was itching to know what it was. The lady behind the counter was bemused that we didn't know what taffy was, but was more than delighted to tell us.

"It's candy with different flavours," she said proudly.

"But, why's it called Salt Water Taffy?" I asked.

"I don't know, I'm afraid," she replied.

I wonder if she knows about the San Andreas Fault.

Buying a bag of the taffy, I was looking forward to trying it.

I would say it's sort of a soft toffee, all different flavours, hence the bright colours, and with a hint of salt. It was quite yummy. Anyway, I had to find out why this candy is called *Salt Water Taffy*. The story goes that, in 1883, a sweetie shop owner called Bradley, had his shop flooded during a storm; all his taffy was soaked with seawater.

He decided to call it *Salt Water Taffy* as a joke and, as with many of these things, it became popular in coastal towns in the US.

Hmmmm, I wonder how our seaside sticks of rock got its name?

Leaving the main US-101 Highway and heading inland, you discover the Lost Coast Road; a 100-mile stretch of un-developed California. The name *Lost Coast* was too intriguing not to explore, so that's the way we headed. I'm glad we did as the scenery was quite beautiful. The rugged and wild landscape of this part of California proved too costly for any major routes to be built. It's quite nice when nature has the upper hand. This almost forgotten road had surprises around every corner, including and, without warning, gravel, hair-pin bends/switchback and steep inclines! These are all fine if you're expecting them. Up on the pegs, fully loaded, I followed Mike down the gravelled, stony road.

On a sharp hairpin bend, I saw that Mike had pulled over into the side. *What the hell*?? I was going to keep going but Mike shouted, *"We'll stop here and have some lunch."*

That's good enough for me! Crawling to a stop, my tummy was already growling. Who doesn't like a picnic? Well, I guess there will be folk who prefer to sit indoors rather than dining alfresco, and why not? But me, I love picnics; I always have. Each place we have stopped on our trip to eat our lunch, has smelled and sounded different.

Here, sitting somewhere on the Lost Coast Road on a gravelly road, I take a deep breath and enjoy the sweet fragrance of the forest around us. Closing my eyes, I soak up the rays of sun filtering through the trees. A slight breeze touches my skin, nature's kiss.

Feeling refreshed, it was time to go onwards and, in this case, downwards! Before heading down the rest of the 'unknown', out came the lipstick. When the going gets tough, apply lipstick!!

Stopping to fuel up in the sleepy little town of Honeydew in Humboldt County, I thought we had landed in the middle of *The Waltons* film set. This was real small-town America and, although not locals, we were greeted like old friends. However, the hippy girl in dungarees sitting outside the general store hitting her head with a plastic spoon was oblivious to us.

Forget *The Waltons*, I think it's more like *Beverly Hillbillies!*

Five minutes after leaving The Lost Coast Road, we found ourselves in the charming Victorian town of Ferndale. The quirky town known as one of America's prettiest towns has a charm of its own. Interestingly, we discovered that the entire town has been designated a historical landmark in the State of California.

Camping on the outskirts of the Ferndale cost us the princely sum of $5 which meant that we could splash out on a meal in town. Taking a leisurely stroll from our tent into the town, gave us the chance to admire the picture-perfect homes and hotels, each one with its own unique charm. Looking back on our time in the States, it's the small towns like Ferndale that I have the fondest memories of; not Houston or Las Vegas. How many tourists visit these big cities and think that this is the real America?

Question: how can two motorcycles ride 106 miles in a straight line and end up only 20 miles away from where they started??? Confused?

Answer: One of the two riders left their kindle charging in the campsite!

So we had to ride +40 miles back to where we started from!

Mike has a habit of misplacing (losing) or forgetting his

belongings. Each time he got on his bike, I would check he had his bum bag with passports etc on him, and sometimes I would ride alongside him to see if it was there. Now, I have to make sure that he's got his kindle!

My work here is never done.

Lynn Aitken

The only way
is up!

The Greek word for *I have found it!* 'Eureka'. I wonder if this word was hollered in excitement by a Gold Rush miner when he discovered a large nugget. I can't imagine driving into a town called, *'I have found it!'* Far better to say that we've arrived in Eureka!

Staying overnight in Eureka wasn't part of the plan, but having to ride back to retrieve Mike's Kindle ate into our day. It made sense to call it quits and book into a hotel in Eureka; tomorrow's another day.

I'm glad we did stop; if we had ridden by Eureka, we would not have discovered the *Black Lightning Motorcycle Cafe* and met owners, Cassandra and Jeff Hesseltine.

The cafe is an informal place where you can buy riding gear, have a bite to eat and enjoy a coffee in a proper cup (no polystyrene!!) as well as a chance to meet and chat with other riding buddies. Looking around the cafe, I noticed some photographs on the wall with a biker *on the limit of lean*, obviously on a racing track.

Cassandra saw me looking at the photos, *"That's Jeff,"* she said.

"Your Jeff?"

Smiling, Cassandra replied, *"Yes, he was an AFM racer."*

Seeing my confused look, she added, *"American Federation of Motorcyclists."*

I was suitably impressed and slightly envious; I would love to be able to lean over on a bend and scrap my knees on the ground (wearing knee pads, of course and on a race track!). I have scraped my pegs at Knockhill Race Track and it was thrilling and scary at the same time!

'A good traveller has no fixed plans, and is not intent on arriving' - Lao Tzu

From Eureka, the aim was to cut east for about a 1000 miles to Yellowstone National Park. However, having checked the weather over in the park, -26 degrees Celsius overnight and highs of -6 during the day; there was no way we could visit this time. Spring hasn't quite reached Yellowstone, but I'm sure it's knocking on the door. For us early travellers, we'll leave Yellowstone sleeping under a blanket of snow and follow spring.

Thank goodness for the national parks is what I would like to say. They protect places like this, the Redwood National Park. From a seed no bigger than one from a tomato, grows the world's tallest trees, the coastal Redwoods of California. Growing to heights of 367 feet (112 m) and widths of 22 feet (7 m) at the base, the Redwoods towered above us.

Gazing up, Mike whispered, "*Honey, I shrunk the kids,*"

"*Why are we whispering?*" I whispered back

Mike didn't answer, he didn't have to. We were in a magical place centuries old and the tranquillity of the forest washed over us. Nothing else for it but to hug one of these majestic trees and that's exactly what Mike did. Ah, you thought it would be me hugging the tree, didn't you? Following suit, I did just that, but Mike hugged the tree first; just putting that out there!

The bark, rough against my face, I closed my eyes and breathed deeply. How lucky we were to experience this, far from the pressures and stresses of modern day life. Would I rather be sitting in heavy traffic hardly moving or in the office staring at a computer screen than here, in this ancient forest? With the only sounds being that of a gentle breeze whispering through the pines, it was a no brainer.

With all the miles we were covering, our tyres would have to be changed at some point and Mike's bike being bigger and carrying more weight (sorry Mike!!), needed new tyres sooner.

Camping in Klamath, only 21 miles south of Crescent City, We found a place in the city, itself, where we could get the right tyres fitted. Normally, you would expect a garage or bike dealer and that's what we were looking out for. The directions took us, however, down a bumpy, dirt track to a shed, a big shed, but a shed nonetheless. The 'reception' was an armchair, a small table and a shotgun! I think quibbling about the price would be a non-starter!

"*What are you doing? Put the camera away Mike!!*"

Focusing his camera on the shotgun, "*I've got to get a photo of this,*" he replied excitedly. This husband of mine was going to get us shot!

The gun, it seems, was only there in case next door's Pit Bull got loose -YEAH RIGHT!!

We didn't argue about the price!

Are we so distracted during the day, that we don't hear the sounds around us, or does sound travel farther at night? The last night in California, tucked up in our sleeping bags, we lay listening to the lapping of waves onto sand. Then, just as we were drifting off to sleep, the hoot of an owl close by, stirred us awake.

"*Aw, do you think she's calling her mate?*" I asked sleepily

"*Too-wit too-woo,*" Mike called out.

"*Too-wit too-woo,*" the owl answered

"*Too-wit too-woo,*" replied Mike.

This is going to be a long night! I thought.

Mike's a man of few words, the strong, silent type, unless he's having a conversation with an owl!! I have no idea what they were saying to each other, but it went on for quite a while!!

THE BEAVER STATE

Fun Fact: *There are more ghost towns in Oregon than any other state in the USA.*

I will have to; at some point count how many States in the US that we've ridden through! Goodbye California, hello Oregon, the Beaver State.

Oregon's Pacific coastline is quite stunning with jagged rock formations all different shapes and sizes. Keeping eyes on the road, I managed to steal glances towards the breathtakingly beautiful coastline.

Soon, we were gazing up at sandy mountains; *this must be the Oregon Dunes*, I thought, with a tinge of excitement.

We found a lovely KOA campsite right by Oregon Sand Dunes. Riding into the site, ATVs (All Terrain Vehicles/dune buggies) were driving here and there. The tinge of excitement I felt was growing; ATVs and sand dunes meant fun was to be had!

Tent set up, I noticed, again that we were the only folk with tents. *Do the Americans not camp?*

Our neighbour popped over to say hi. She talked out the side of her mouth with a southern drawl, asking us where we were headed.

"All the way to Alaska," I replied, while still hardly believing that we were actually riding to Alaska!

She asked *"How y'all gonna get there?"*

"Through Canada," we replied in unison.

"Re..a....lly?"

"Yes, Alaska is above Canada!" Mike informed her.

Who said that sarcasm is the ability to insult idiots without them realising?

The Oregon dunes can tower up to 500 feet above sea level and the geography changes with the wind, literally.

Trying to save money by camping most of the time allows us to spend a little on activities or places we visit, so we could afford to have some fun riding the dunes in ATVs. What could possibly go wrong? This would be swapping two wheels for four wheels driving on a bit of sand.

Having been given some training on how to operate an ATV and staying safe, (emphasis on 'safe'!) we were off.

Trundling along the dirt track, we soon arrived at the dunes.

If you've ever been on a roller coaster, you'll know there's the climbing up and up to the top of the hill, then that moment of, *Oh shit, why the hell did I do this?,* knowing that it's too late; you're committed and there's nothing you can do about it but hold on and accept your fate.

That just about describes riding the dunes, except the driving up to the top has to be as fast as the ATV will go and then, at the top, you stop and realise that you have to go down and it's a lot steeper than it looked from the bottom.

It's eye-popping fun! Mike went over the edge first and there was nothing for it but to follow.

At the bottom, I came to a stop by Mike and his ATV. Looking over at him smiling, Mike yelled over the noise of the engines, "*Wow! That was crazy. Let's do it again!!*"

And off we went ....no, we're not adrenalin junkies (much!!)

Mike's enthusiasm quite often outweighs his ability! He's a typical squaddie (soldier) and I love that he is. Our children have that same enthusiasm for life.

They grew up building dens and climbing trees, knowing that it was OK to come home muddy. Walking through the woods, our boys, Vaughan and Daryl can still remember where their bases were. Hazel was too young to play there, but today she loves walking Brodie, our dog, in the woods armed with a camera.

Back to Mike's enthusiasm versus ability. Going downhill, he thought he would get well ahead of me, do a sharp turn and video me driving down towards him. Sounds like a plan? The only video recorded, with sound effects I hasten to add, was Mike turning sharply, rolling his ATV, face planting the sand and cracking his ribs!

Seeing this all play out in front of me, it seemed to take ages to reach Mike.

Running over to him, Mike was still lying on the sand, groaning; I knew this could be serious.

Together, we managed to push the ATV upright, Mike holding his ribs. Having cracked ribs in the past, he knew that's what he had just done.

This could have been a painful end to the trip but, thankfully, Mike was able to continue, albeit with cracked ribs. Sneezing or coughing to be avoided, but farting's OK! An interesting thing we found out, though, was that camping was better for his ribs than proper beds.

WASHINGTON; THE EVERGREEN STATE

It was time to leave Oregon and discover Washington, the Evergreen State. A 4.1 mile ride over the Columbia River via the Astoria-Megler Bridge and we arrived in Washington.

Being an ex-Engineer, Mike used to build bridges and still to this day, is fascinated by them. He sees the technical side, how these structures were put together. I like the different shapes and sizes and this bridge, connecting the two states, is quite impressive and, for me, more memorable than the Golden Gate Bridge in San Francisco.

Whilst writing this during a quiet moment at work in our little ticket hut, I showed Daniel, my colleague pictures of the Astoria-Megler Bridge and asked how he would describe it.

After yawning, Daniel replied, *"It looks like a metal hill."*

Hmmm, that's the best answer I'm going to get out of Daniel at 3:30 on a hot afternoon!

We, or rather Mike, put a lot of thought and research into the kit we would need to take. With items such as sleeping bags and the tent, we decided to go for quality and it paid off. However even with quality kit, things can still go wrong, and it was the inner tent zip which broke.

Thoughts of Alaska and the monster mosquitoes we had been warned about, meant that to have a sleeping compartment that we could zip up was vital. The good news is that when something does go wrong with quality equipment, there's usually guarantees and support from the seller.

After contacting Redverz, their answer was, "*No problem, we'll replace it asap.*"

"*What's your address?*" they continued

Great, we could get a replacement, but an address? We're nomads at the moment; no fixed abode.

"*That shouldn't be a problem,*" was their reply.

Really? we thought.

The company had a plan. They could send it to one of their distributing agents in the vicinity that we were travelling through. Arranging, en-route, where we could collect the replacement inner compartment, we decided on Tacoma on the outskirts of Seattle.

Seattle, another city. Is it awful that we didn't even venture into Seattle? I've decided that I'm more of a country gal than city lass. I know that a famous coffee brand comes from Seattle though!

Staying away from the city, we found another KOA campsite in Tacoma itself. Still too built up for our liking, but we desperately needed that inner compartment.

This campsite was a far cry from the other KOA sites we had stayed at. Here, it seemed to be housing homeless folk and the site itself was pretty run down looking. Our fellow campers, although down on their luck, were welcoming and friendly. They had an excuse to moan and complain, but they seemed happy with their lot. Or, maybe the wacky backy helped! The unmistakable, heavy odour of cannabis wafted through the campsite.

In the tent next to ours were a couple of guys and their small dog, Boo. One of the men was severely disabled and confined to a motorised wheelchair, his face all bruised after falling out of his chair. I felt heart sorry for him. What a way to live in this day and age. Reflecting on Tacoma and the disabled man, I'm wondering what became of him and his dog, Boo; something nice I hope.

Riding out of Tacoma and the campsite, It took a while to shake off that sad feeling gnawing at me about Boo and his owners.

If we had checked into a comfortable hotel, we would never have met them and witnessed these real human stories, away from all the glitz and glamour of the tourist destinations.

How could I stay sad when I gazed up in awe at the majestic and snowy Mount Rainier which dominates the skyline around Seattle? One of the world's largest volcanoes, Mount Rainier is nearly three miles high and is the tallest peak in the Cascade Range. Coming from Scotland, I feel at home surrounded by mountains. They stand defiant against the elements all the while, looking down upon us.

A number of years ago, we were on the Italian coast and chose to leave the crowds on the beaches to climb a hill; I don't think it was classed as a mountain but it was still quite high. The only people at the top, we sat on a rock enjoying the coolness of the mountain air, eating our picnic, all was quiet around us and yet, we could hear the voices and noises drifting up from the beach and town. I felt like we had escaped to a much nicer and peaceful place. Since then, when I look up at the hills, I imagine them listening to us daft humans with our chaotic lives.

A detour up Mount Rainier, although tempting, would have been exhilarating, but the mountain was sleeping under a blanket of snow and ice and the roads remained closed.

Our ride from Tacoma should have been just 150 miles; our destination, a campsite in Leavenworth. The road, as scenic as it was, wasn't as twisty as we thought it would be. The route took us up and through Stevens Pass, a ski resort, so thank goodness we were dressed for the cold. It's quite surreal to be riding along and seeing skiers on either side of the road. The temperature had plummeted and the biting cold meant that the heated grips were on once more.

Dropping elevation, we were soon leaving the snow behind, the air warming up and the feeling gradually coming back to my fingers. The heated grips are great, however it's only the palms of the hands that benefit from the warmth. I now have bar muffs on my handlebars; my hands are always warm now and I wouldn't be without them.

We reached the town of Leavenworth, Washington, but this could have been a town in the Bavarian Alps with its wooden balconies and painted timber. Having lived for many years in Germany, Bavaria (Bayern) was one of our favourite holiday destinations. Leavenworth must surely have links to Bavaria, or did it? The town, as it is today, is completely deliberate and a 'do-or-die' attempt to save the town.

Leavenworth flourished until the Great Northern Railway abandoned the town in favour of a new route which was more efficient, especially during the winter.

The railroad leaving almost sealed Leavenworth's fate, the town was slowly dying. Perhaps it was the alpine feel of the area surrounding Leavenworth which gave the town officials the ingenious idea of creating a Bavarian town. Whatever it was, the birth of a Bavarian town in Washington State, complete with German festivals and nutcrackers, has quite simply saved the community.

It was too early in the day to stop so we rode on by, admiring this charming mountain town from the seats of our bikes. With hindsight, I wish we had stopped in Leavenworth for the night and reminisce about our time in Germany. Perhaps even find a traditional Bavarian bakery selling warm, salted, chewy Brezeln (pretzels) to eat as we browsed around the shops.

But, then again, would we have judged Leavenworth unfairly, comparing it to the Germany we have fond memories of? Who knows.

Leaving the beauty of the snow-capped mountains, it wasn't long until we found ourselves in a flat wilderness which turned out to be 'crop circle' country. The change in landscape was quite sudden and dramatic. Gone was the freshness of the mountains, replaced by an eerie and haunting atmosphere; even the skies had darkened. Looking around, I found the area oppressive and could see why folk believed that aliens visited here; there was just something not quite right with the place. Creepy is a good word to describe it.

IDAHO; THE GEM STATE

Mention Idaho and some may think of potatoes, and, indeed, the State is famous for its potatoes. There is, however, a fun fact I read about Idaho. It is forbidden to give another citizen a box of candy (sweets) weighing more than 50 pounds in Idaho. Who on earth would ever give someone a box of candy weighing more than 50 pounds, or even close to that? And how did this become illegal? Had this been a common problem in Idaho?

One of the fun parts of the trip and a necessity to keep costs down, was enjoying a picnic each day to eat by the side of the road. To be able to plan a picnic or BBQ with good weather in Scotland is quite a luxury so this was a bit of a novelty, albeit an enjoyable one.

At times, we hadn't had the chance to put together a picnic, so the only thing for it was to stop at cafes along the way, which usually happened to be non-franchise diners. Far from flashy looking, these individual diners were great and part of the whole *American experience*. The moment we sat down, there's a friendly server pouring a much needed coffee in a proper cup, I may add. Next is the menu; this is grandma's cooking. Delicious home cooking and nothing is too much trouble and there's always refills of coffee.

I'm sure my coffee intake was greatly increased from when we're at home.

Looking at the menu one day in a cosy little diner, Mike

asked the waitress, "*What's biscuits and gravy?*"

The waitress was flabbergasted that we had no idea what it was. To us, biscuits are sweet and we usually dunk them in a cup of tea; and gravy is something that goes over mashed tatties (potatoes!).

"*You guys don't know what biscuits and gravy is?*" she asked.

OK, now the whole diner knew that we were definitely not from around these here parts! People stopped eating and chatting to look over at us!

"*Oh you gotta try biscuits and gravy. It's biscuits with gravy,*" she added.

That really didn't help, so no more the wiser and rather than looking more daft than we did already, Mike replied,

"*Well, I guess I'll try the biscuits and gravy*"

Being a strict vegetarian, I had a feeling that this was going to be non-veggie, so to stay on the safe side and not to shock the poor lady anymore, I ordered French toast with maple syrup. To this day, I still put maple syrup on my French toast; delicious!

The maple syrup has to be the best on the supermarket shelves though; I guess I'm a maple syrup snob!

The biscuits and gravy? Mike's expression said it all; warm, mouth-watering comfort food and something he ordered regularly the rest of the trip.

So, we were in Idaho, but where? We had been to so many places that, sometimes it was all a blur. Thank you, Ivy for that calendar!! I still refer to the calendar to remind myself of where we were and when.

Sitting in the camp site, somewhere in Idaho, and before I had a chance to update my calendar, Mike asked, "*Where are we?*"

"*What does it start with?*" I asked. Now this is a system I rely on. I find going through the alphabet helps!! It works for me anyway.

"*I don't know,*" he replied. My system wouldn't work if we didn't even know what it started with!

We didn't even know which town we were in! Before having to actually walk out of the campsite to find a town sign, I tried the alphabet,

"Right, let's give it a go. A, B......Bonners Ferry, that's where we are!"

MONTANA; BIG SKY COUNTRY

Texas, Arizona, Nevada, California........I feel like we were 'bagging' States! In fact, I have lost track of exactly how many States we've been through. Each one, like the national parks, is different and unique. They are almost like separate countries, each with their own history, culture, and geography. I guess that's why a lot of Americans don't have passports; they have everything from desert to mountains to the coast; no need to travel abroad.

Our next State to 'bag' was Montana, home to Glacier National Park, also known as the *Crown of the Continent*. I don't know why it's known as this, but I like to think that the snow capped mountain peaks is the crown.

Heading into the town of Kalispell, we set up camp in a spotlessly clean campsite which, I have to say was the best up to now. We've stayed at so many campsites on this trip, each offering different facilities that I think we could set up one of our own and know what works and what doesn't. Hmmm, maybe a future business venture for us?

Camping has to be, for me, one of the highlights of the trip; our home is wherever we decide to stop. Booking into a hotel in Kalispell would have meant missing the busy campsite woodpecker, our neighbour. He spent his day building a nest, a home, in the hope of attracting a mate.

Every now and then, he would have a wee tidy around, come out of his nest, which was a hole in the tree, and call out to all those pretty female woodpeckers out there. Who could resist a guy who builds the home and cleans up as well? I do hope all that effort hasn't been in vain.

In Kalispell for a few days would give us the opportunity to catch up with a bit of admin; washing, shopping and doing a bit of maintenance on the bikes. We were also both in desperate need of a haircut which meant a trip downtown to historic Kalispell.

With the mountains of Glacier as a backdrop, the small town of Kalispell, with its restored 1800s buildings, is really quite quaint. It was easy to spot the barbers with its red, white and blue pole outside one of the historic buildings.

The young barber, who owned the shop, was clearly passionate about his trade. Chatting to him while he cut Mike's hair, we discovered that the shop had been a barber for years and he wanted to keep its 'old ways' which included being offered soda, beer or whisky (I can't bring myself to put the *e* in whisky......sorry our American friends) Mike enjoyed a pampering which ended with a neck massage. Ladies, when our men folk go to the barbers, don't be fooled. They're in there for ages being spoilt! And guys who go and pay extra in a hairdressers, you're being conned! Stick with the barbers!!

My turn for a haircut; miles of riding through deserts and the like, my hair was like straw. As soon as I put my bike helmet on, my head would start itching. I tried argan oil which helped for a short time, but after an hour of riding, I wanted to scratch my head but couldn't. Since coming home, I've heard that this is quite common.

Anyway, my hair! No luck for me finding a hairdresser

without an appointment so, Mike looking great after his pampering and me looking like I've been dragged through the proverbial hedge backwards, we headed back to the campsite.

In Kalispell, we were basking in summer temperatures and yet, just 20 miles away, a lot of Glacier National Park was still closed due to the snow. At least we would be able to see some of Glacier and, wow, what a breathtakingly beautiful park.

The tranquillity with so few people was rather pleasant, or is it that I might be slightly unsociable?
Parking the bikes, we donned our walking kit to go for a hike up to the snow line. The warmth of the sun beating down on us and the chill of the snow underfoot, reminded me of our hikes in Germany when spring was knocking on the door giving winter the heave ho.

After our hike, it was still early in the day so time to have a fun ride. With no particular destination in mind, we discovered an unpaved and dusty road....very dusty indeed, especially when I'm riding behind Mike eating the dirt he's kicking up!

Our time in Kalispell had been amazing. There was a crisp, clean feel to this region and we were sad to leave, but leave we must if we want to get to our destination which is still the last frontier, Alaska.

Our last night in the campsite meant take a shower because you never knew when the next wash would be. I had just entered the shower block when a lady walked in after me. Thinking nothing of it, I jumped into the shower. As the hot water washed over me, I heard a voice chatting away in the next cubicle. I was pretty certain that there was only me and the other lady in the shower block. When she launched into grunting and other weird noises, I started feeling slightly uneasy. Actually, I was freaked out to be honest!

I have a vivid imagination and the film, *Psycho* by Alfred Hitchcock popped into my head along with famous sound effects from the shower scene! Cutting (wrong choice of word!) my shower short, I quickly dried myself and stepped out of the cubicle only to see Miss Psycho's head with dripping hair poking out of her shower cubicle, looking at me.

Cackling, she asked *"Like my singing huh?"*

That was me out of there without even cleaning my teeth!!

Mike likes to be the "Feuermeister" (he who is in charge of the fire).....is it a 'man' thing or am I being sexist? On our last morning in Montana, I woke up early and, straight away, felt the chill in the air. Breathing gently and rhythmically beside me, Mike was still in the 'land of nod'. I could snuggle up to him and doze for a while or get up, surprise him by lighting a fire and making breakfast. Now fully awake, I quietly dressed and crawled out of the tent, shivering when the frosty air hit me. Looking back at Mike all warm and cosy, I was tempted to climb back into bed and join him. But then, spotting lots of pine cones on the ground, I had a bit of an epiphany! Taking a brown paper bag, I gathered up some of the dryer cones, popped them into the bag which I then used as a fire-starter. It worked a treat and even Mike admitted that it was a good idea but, and there's always a *But* with my hubbie. *"But, why light a fire in the morning?"* I can't win!!

After breakfast by my little fire, we packed up camp and left Kalispell via a stunning road which skirted around Glacier. Riding along looking up at the snow-capped mountains set against a bluer than blue sky, I wondered how I would describe Montana to folk back home. The air, crisp and with a hint of pine, towering mountains, shimmering lakes and big blue skies; I could be describing Austria or Switzerlan.

Following a map, we soon arrived at the start of a short cut we had been told about. If we took this road, it was eight miles. Taking the long way round would be forty miles. A no brainer, we thought, until we saw a barrier partially blocking the road entrance, which read, *Road Closed*

"What do you think, Mike?"

"Well, it looks like the sign's been moved to let traffic through. I think we should go for it," he decided.

"OK, why not, how bad can it be? It could be that they've just forgotten to remove the sign" I agreed.

After eight miles of riding slowly along a twisting, narrow mountain road, zigzagging around rock falls, we both admitted that the Pass was probably still closed after all! The smiles on our faces said it all; this was living.

That's the road we're taking!

CANADA; GREAT WHITE NORTH

Crossing the border into Canada was the smoothest yet. Hardly any questions, a quick stamp in our passports and we were on our way into another country. Leaving the mountains of Glacier National Park behind us, immediately, the terrain changed to prairie like countryside with buffalo grazing. Looking back towards Montana and the US, the strange tower shaped mountain standing alone, *Old Chief Mountain* bid us farewell.

Miles turned to kilometres; we had definitely left the USA, for now anyway. Although I was looking forward to the next part of our journey, the flat landscape all around us was having a negative effect on me, for sure. Is this the Scot in me?

The first town we stopped at was Cardston, Alberta. The only campsite was closed even though it was meant to be open from April, weather permitting. The weather was 20 degrees so I'm wondering how hot it has to be!! So, a motel it would have to be.

The low feeling was still there and it wasn't just the change in landscape. Although we had been on the road for a while now, I still had the days when I felt down and ache of missing my family intensified.

I just needed to let it run its course and give myself a kick up the butt. I would be seeing my family soon and I knew they were excited for us to make the most of this chance of adventure.

My mood continued on a downward spiral when we stopped at the only place in town for lunch and they didn't seem to know about vegetarians. That's fine, I'm used to grabbing what I can.

Looking up at the menu, Mike ordered a burger.

"Hi, do you have anything vegetarian?" I asked.

"We have a small side salad mam," the rather stout attendant offered.

"Oh, OK, I'll have that, please, and a bun (roll)."

"We don't have buns mam," he replied.

Looking bemused at the mountain of burger buns on the counter behind him, I tried again,

"What about one of those buns on the counter?"

"I'm sorry mam, they're only for burgers."

"But I'm vegetarian, so could I just have one bun, please, to go with the salad?"

"No, mam, I'm sorry, that's not on the menu."

If he called me 'mam' one more time, I would probably lose it! Yep, my tolerance was extremely low at this particular moment, especially for a 'jobs-worth'.

Keeping my cool, I grabbed my salad, paid and scowled.

I wish I had asked for a burger with the bun at the side, paid, and then handed him the burger back, saying, *"I've got the bun, you can have the burger back!"* Hindsight is a great thing!

My hair was getting the better of me, it wasn't how it looked, and believe me it was pretty bad. No, it was the intense itching whenever I put my helmet on. It was quite literally driving me mad.

We were staying overnight in a motel with internet access, so I decided to plan ahead and search, online, for hairdressers in the next town we would be travelling through, Raymond.

Success! I found a hairdresser and made an appointment; time to have this mop; I call 'hair', sorted.

Not wanting to appear desperate, but the next day, we arrived in Raymond slightly early for my hair appointment.

With plenty of time, we asked one of the townsfolk where we could go for a coffee,

"Oh, I don't know, you see our coffee lady passed away."

When she saw the look on my face, she explained, *"Raymond is 95% Mormon who don't drink coffee, so there's no call for a cafe."*

I'm just putting this out there so bear with me. If all these people get to Heaven, is God going to say, *"Thank you for not drinking coffee, you can enter the house of God!"*

I couldn't have a coffee but I could get a haircut. Turns out, I had my hair done and enjoyed a coffee. The hairdresser was Mormon but she offered coffee to clients, all 5% of them. Relaxing with my coffee and happy to watch the hairdresser work her magic with my hair, I relaxed.

"So, the UK isn't an island is it? It's on the edge of Europe isn't it?" she asked me.

This was going to be more interesting than the usual hairdresser chit chat, *"Are you going anywhere nice on holiday?"* or *"any plans for going out tonight?"*

"Yes, we're an island, but we're still part of Europe," I replied, trying to keep a straight and serious face.

"I didn't know that," she continued, *"it's been a long time since I took Social Studies."*

I wasn't prepared for what she said next. *"I'd like to visit Europe but not sure 'cos of all those Muslims killing people."*

Political correctness, this was not. She was a nice enough lass, so I corrected her in the nicest possible way. That didn't stop her though; she was on a roll.

Unable to run away, I sat listening to her drone on, *"Y'know, those politicians running Canada now aren't listening to us in Alberta. And our Prime Minister should be shot!"* said this most religious person.

"And the schools don't listen to the parents. It's all about transgender children. If a boy wants to be a girl and tells their teacher, the school won't let the parents know. I'm not against queers or anything but......"

I just hope she doesn't leave Raymond is all I'm thinking!! She's safe here, they know her!

Feeling incredible with my new hairdo, I almost skipped out of the most surreal hairdressing appointment I have ever had! We were just about ready to leave the town of Raymond, when a Peace Officer, aka, law enforcement, drove slowly by eyeing up our bikes.

"He's coming back," I whispered to Mike.

"Hey there folks, where you guys from?" he asked.

Today was getting more and more kooky. The Officer noticed Mike's 'Blue Knight' stickers and it turned out that he worked alongside another member of the international police motorcycle club. Before we knew it, there were two police cars beside us and another police officer, the Blue Knight. For this small town, we were something to curtain twitch about. As we were chatting to the officer, there was a small crowd gathering opposite. Thinking back to the earlier conversations in the hairdressers, I was wondering what the townsfolk had decided we were.

After we said our goodbyes to the Police Officers, we still had one more thing to get in Raymond before leaving. We were on our way to our niece-in-law's parents, Vanessa and Kerry near Foremost. Space is always tight on a trip like this but we couldn't turn up to someone's house empty handed. I wanted to buy a box of chocolates. You would think that this would be easy, but we were still in Raymond!

Nipping into one of the few shops in Raymond to buy chocolates, I couldn't see any so asked the guy at the till,

"Do you have any boxes of chocolates?

"What d'ya mean a box of choc-o-lates?" he replied in a *'Forest Gump'* drawl.

By this time, I was wondering if we were on candid camera!

"Chocolates in a box," I confirmed whilst trying to maintain composure.

"I don't know whatcha mean," (same *'Forest Gump'* drawl!)

"Biscuits, I'll just have these biscuits, thanks!"

Mike had been waiting outside by the bikes, *"I thought you were getting chocolates?"* he asked. Time to leave!

Following Vanessa's brilliant directions, we reached Foremost. The next bit would be tricky, Vanessa had warned us. The road leading to their house was a few miles of gravel. *"No problem,"* we said confidently, especially after riding in

Mexico.

I love the thrill of riding off road, but there's two types of surface I'd rather steer clear of........ice and gravel.....oh and sand....that makes three.Keeping to the best of the track and up on the pegs, we started down the gravel road. Minutes later, a cheeky patch of deeper gravel got the better of me and I was plummeting off the road down into a deep ditch. Thinking back, I can't remember being scared when my motorcycle and I parted company, just the feeling of tumbling over and over.

Coming to a stop some way from my bike, my mind automatically 'scanned' my body for injuries. Everything seemed OK, some pain but I was alive. Crawling over to my bike, I switched off the ignition. My poor bike looked sorry for herself and I thought *SHIT!!*

That's when I got angry. Angry that I had come off, angry that I had lost control, angry that my bike was pretty damaged and angry that my panniers were strewn all over the place. But most of all, I was scared and just wanted to go home before something serious happened and I didn't see my family again. Is this trip really worth that??

Mike laughs when I lose my temper; apparently I'm a funny angry person! But he wasn't here to see this paddy; he hadn't seen me disappear into a ditch. So, how does a funny angry person have a paddy?

I picked up my wing mirror and chucked it, I picked up my indicator and chucked that and then I sat down and cried. How must I have looked crawling up the embankment out of the ditch covered in dust? And, where was Mike?

Shouting and stomping my feet, "*He's left me! He's bloody left me!! Right that's it,*" I said, picking up my panniers and putting them down again, for no reason at all.

Turns out that Mike had come off his bike further up the road. He had ridden down into a *coulee*, hence why I couldn't see him. Caitlyn, our niece-in-law had told us about the coulees on the land around her home. Looking ahead, the ground looks flat but the coulees are hidden gullies which appear as you get up to them. It was at the bottom of one that Mike had come off his bike, again in deep gravel. Both invisible from each other and Mike must have been wondering where I was. Unlike my panniers which pop off if I topple, Mike's sturdy panniers stay on which meant that he had to take them off before picking up his bike, as it would have been too heavy otherwise.

Foremost is a small community and everyone knows each other, so when a truck stopped by and asked if he could help, he also called Kerry and Vanessa to let them know what had happened. Before we knew it, Kerry was there in his truck with one of his farm hands. I managed to start my bike and, between us all, we pushed it up and out of the ditch, loading the bike, via a wooden ramp, onto the back of the truck along with all the bits and bobs I had chucked.

I was mortified; Kerry hadn't been well at all and the last thing we wanted to do was be a burden. We were looking forward to staying with Kerry and Vanessa a couple of nights, catch up and lend a hand at this busy seeding time on the farm. Well, this put paid to all of that!

Arriving at the house, Vanessa greeted us with a lovely hug and immediately, I felt slightly better. It was really nice to be able to visit Caitlyn's family and get to know them as we had only briefly met them at Tim and Caitlyn's wedding. After a delicious meal with Vanessa, Kerry, grandmother Ruby and other family members, I started feeling sore and stiff.

My ankle was swelling up fast, was it broken? I wasn't going to mention it but When Vanessa saw me limping, she wanted to take me for an X ray but there was no way I was going to be any more of a burden than I already felt.

Hobbling and holding onto Mike and Vanessa, I went to bed keeping my foot raised with ice on it.

We woke up the next morning to the delicious smell of homemade flapjacks being cooked, or what we call pancakes. This is a traditional Canadian breakfast and one that I could get used to. No porridge for us today!

I still couldn't put any weight onto my foot, but with Mike's help, I managed to get upstairs. It would take more than a 'could be' broken ankle to come between me and homemade pancakes!

After breakfast, I called *Blackfoot Motors* in Calgary to see if they could repair Trixie. They had a two month waiting list, but will always help travelling motorcyclists if they can, so their answer was "*Yes!*"

Kerry very kindly offered us his truck so that we could drive the bike 200 miles to Calgary. Off we went with my foot raised up on the dashboard.

Trixie would be fixed by the next day so we booked into a hotel for the night and a couple of glasses of wine later, helped dull the ache in my ankle.

The guys at Blackfoot Motors were brilliant and my bike was looking a lot better. She was sporting new fancy handle bars and her other parts 'sewn' together with cable ties and glue. She was going home battle scarred.

As well as the damage, my tyres were about ready for changing so we decided that I should get better, knobbly ones for riding off road, but would still be good for roads. Alaska, bring it on!!

But first, the 200 mile drive back to Foremost and Vanessa and Kerry's.
Again, I felt humbled by the warmth and kindness shown to us by this lovely couple. After dinner, Kerry asked smiling, "*Would you be partial to a rum and coke?*" We felt truly honoured. Relaxing with a rum and coke, the four of us sat chatting until late into the evening; an evening I will always remember.

The following day, the telephone lines around Foremost were buzzing. It had rained overnight just after the farmers, including Kerry, had planted the seeds. This was good news indeed and we found ourselves carried along by the excitement. We go to the supermarket and expect to be able to buy our food grown on farms like Kerry and Vanessa's. How often do we think about the farmer who planted the seeds and hoped for the right amount of rain, warmth and sunshine for the crops to grow?

Did Kerry's enthusiasm rub off on me? I don't know, but, this year I've started growing a few of my own vegetables. It's an amazing feeling to see something grow from a tiny seed that I planted and then to dish it up in a meal.

The next morning, I managed to squeeze my foot into my bike boot, even though I couldn't fasten it shut. Hey ho, at least I could ride my bike.

We said our goodbyes to Kerry and Vanessa and headed to Calgary, stopping for a cuppa at Ruby's, Kerry's mum. She's an amazing lady, so much energy and kindness. Whilst at Ruby's, we met more of Caitlyn's family including her brother, Colton. I had mixed emotions leaving Ruby's. Excited to be on our journey of discovery again but quite sad to be leaving this amazing family who had welcomed us so warmly.

We were on our own again and off to Calgary. Time for a spot of camping and the sun was shining. I had packed my winter jacket and sent it to a friend in Calgary, ready for the colder weather we would surely be riding into. This was something I wish I hadn't done. With postage and then sending my summer jacket back home, it would have been cheaper to take an all-weather jacket. However, we live and learn.

On the plus side, it was lovely to see Steph again who had invited us to a family gathering which proved to be a house full of Scots....surreal.

Apart from some 'admin', relaxing and a bit of shopping, mainly for camping stuff; the only touristy day we had was a visit to Drumheller which is home to the *Royal Tyrrell Museum* housing the world's largest display of dinosaurs.

The 110 km ride from Calgary was, for the most part, flat and boring until we reached Drumheller itself. The terrain, dead flat, suddenly fell away and we were riding into a prehistoric and almost alien looking terrain. This was Drumheller

Valley in the heart of the Badlands. The sandstone Hoodoos, weirdly shaped rocky structures rising tall, dominating the landscape, reminded me of the old western films. Yes, the ride to get there was boring, but worth it to experience this bewitching land.

The heat in this lunar landscape was quite intense and there was no shelter; we were at the mercy of the sun. In our bike kit, we could only melt in silence until we started heading back towards Calgary, the motion creating a refreshing breeze.

We're back!! Banff was still the bustling lively town we remembered from four years ago. Mount Cascade was there, ever watchful above the town which was buzzing with tourists.

Millions of visitors travel to Banff all year round and the resort thrives as a result of this. Due to the warm weather, one of the campsites on the edge of Banff was open. After choosing our spot, we went about setting up our tent, each of us having our specific jobs. Mike always started by putting the tent up, while I blew up the mattresses etc.

One of the best bits of kit we had was a Snozzle bag! How do I describe it? It's a bag which attaches to the mattress and then you 'catch' the air and squeeze it into the mattress. Hey presto! No electrics, no batteries, no charging and yet so simple and efficient; less to go wrong.

The sun was shining, we were back in Banff and we would be celebrating our 32nd anniversary and thank you to my auntie Nancy for giving us some money to treat ourselves to a meal in a nice restaurant. I can't remember why we fell out, but we did and on our anniversary!

Mike asked later, "*What did we fall out about?*"

Glaring at my beloved, I replied, "*You were being a dick!*"

Looking bemused but obviously wanting to keep the peace, he shrugged, "*Oh, OK.*"

After a hearty breakfast at Melissa's, another favourite eating place from our last visit here, we headed onto Jasper stopping at the Athabasca Glacier on the way.

This is a sad and scary reminder that our climate is changing, and not for the better.

The Glacier, which is one of the 'toes' of the Columbia Icefield is receding at an alarming rate. This has mostly happened in the last century or so. The scientists calculate that the glacier is receding at a rate of five metres a year. That means that, since stopping here four years ago, the glacier has reduced by 20 metres!

When are we going to wake up and take notice of what we're doing to our home, the Earth? If we think about the room we're sitting in at this moment; would we happily sit there with harmful fumes polluting the air? No, we have smoke alarms and carbon monoxide monitors fitted. And yet, we seem to be OK with ruining the very place that is keeping us alive. Well, some of us are saying that we're not OK with that.

Riding into Jasper, the temperature was on the chilly side. What was I saying about climate change??? The cold in Jasper was weather and not climate.

Brrrr! All the campsites were still closed so there was nothing for it but to stay in a hotel for the night. Again, a downside to setting out so early in the season.

Climate is what we expect, weather is what we get.

- Mark Twain

HINTON; WE'VE MADE IT!

Emotions were buzzing as we stopped short of Hinton at the *Scenic Road to Alaska* signpost (the 40). This very spot was where the idea for the trip was born four years ago. That time, we were here with just one bike, a rental Harley, or as Mike called it, a tractor! Now, four years on, standing in the same spot for a photo, we were on our own bikes and were itching to ride in the direction of Alaska after a night in Hinton.

The reason we had previously stayed in Hinton was that it was close to Jasper but not as expensive. Being savvy with our cash then, had paid off as we would not have seen the signpost that led to our adventure.

Standing here, now, at the junction, I could hardly believe that we had ridden from Texas into Mexico and all the way north to Canada. Does that make us adventurers or plain daft? I like to think that we're adventurers, all thanks to Mike. We may fall out on our anniversary of all days, but Mike's the one who made me believe in myself that I could make a trip like this.

I could have stayed at home in Scotland, bruise free, but the old saying that life is no rehearsal is so very true. It's also moving to hear our children saying that they're proud of us for doing this. Hazel also called us absurd and crazy, I know, for sure, that she meant it as a compliment.

Continuing down memory lane, we decided that we would stay in the same hotel we were in four years ago. As we were checking in, we got chatting to the Area Manager and, after hearing about our trip, he upgraded us to a suite. And the suite just happened to have a recliner!! No sooner had we crossed the threshold, Mike had his arse on the recliner and he was not moving! Well, until it was *beer O' clock* and time for some food. Talking of food, where else would we go for a bite to eat but the same restaurant as before. Same restaurant, same booth and the décor hadn't changed but the portion sizes had, thank goodness. The portion of apple crumble I had last time, was the size of a dinner plate! Looking at my pudding in horror, I said, "*I only asked for one portion.*"

The waiter smiled, gave me another spoon and said, "*This is one portion mam, but maybe your husband will help ya*"

I looked desperately over the table at Mike, "*Please say you'd like some apple crumble,*" I pleaded. Even with Mike's help, we couldn't finish the crumble.

Fast forward to 2016, I was hungry and ready! I ordered a salad to keep room for this pudding, determined it wasn't going to beat me but, alas, no more apple crumble. It wasn't a 'big' (pardon the pun) seller so they took it off the menu. Ah well, my waistline was thankful.

The moment was here. Leaving Hinton behind, We turned right onto the *Scenic Route to Alaska*. The build up and anticipation proved to be the most exciting part of the road, as it turned out to be quite boring really, with a lot of oil and logging trucks. In my mind's eye, I envisioned us riding into a wilderness, leaving civilisation behind us but no, it's like the ice road truckers but without the ice. Don't get me wrong, it's still a wilderness, if you take away the trucks.

Just under four hours and we had reached Grand Prairie, in the heart of the Peace Region. I thought that sounded nice, the Peace Region.

Finding the location of the campsite, we rode up to register at the reception. Peeking through the windows, we realised that the office was closed.

A map on the wall, however, showed where the tent area was. Nothing for it but to set up camp and pay in the morning when the office reopened.

The tent site was nice and peaceful, no one else there, however, there were no water or toilets close by. It was a six minute walk to the facilities, we timed it! Good exercise but not so good if needing the toilet in a hurry! A long way for a widdle, but then, at least plenty grassland around us to water!

On the plus side, there was lots of free firewood lying around. A caretaker drove past us and confirmed that we were OK to use the wood and set up our tent. Happy days!

During the night, we lay listening to the sound of train horns in the distance, I love that sound. The other sound we listened to was the rain. Again, it's a lovely feeling being tucked up cosy in bed and hearing the pitter-patter of rain on the tent. That is unless you're only staying one night and then it's awful to pack up a wet tent. Decision was made when we woke up in the morning and it was still raining; we would stay another night.

While Mike was making coffee and breakfast, I took myself off to the reception to register our presence and pay. Walking into the office smiling, I was immediately met by a frosty faced lady.

"Good morning. I'd like to register our tent," I said, still smiling.

Her facial expression remained the same, *"I'm sorry? Our tent site is still closed."*

I explained about our late arrival and one of the caretakers telling us that we were fine to camp. With an annoyed look, she agreed to us being there. I didn't dare mention that their website confirmed that the sites were open all year round!

"That'll be $30 dollars a night," she said.

"Err, that's a bit steep," I replied, feeling braver.

"That's what we've been charging."

"Well, it's a bit pricey for a bit of grass," gosh, I was surprising myself.

This was now a showdown.

Ms Frosty Face raised her eyebrows at me, *"That's the price, I'm afraid."*

Now she was annoying me!

"It's a six minute walk to the toilets."

"Six minutes? I don't think so," she challenged.

I wasn't quitting, *"yes, have you walked it?"*

"Yes, I live here."

Neither of us was ready to back down. But, after a few seconds, Ms Frosty Face walked briskly away to speak with someone and came back, avoiding eye contact.

Yes! I won! We were given $20 dollars off the price.

Walking the six minutes back to the tent, I felt quite elated and, at the same time, a wee bit scared of Ms Frosty Face.

I'm going to avoid her, I thought. That was the plan, but plans, sometimes, need to change and there was nothing else for it but to go back and see Ms Frosty about using the laundry machines.

Deep breath, I can do this!

"Hi again," I said cheerfully walking into the Reception.

Surprisingly, Ms Frosty appeared slightly friendlier. *"Yes, how can I help you?"* she asked, smiling.

Hmm, she must have a double

"I was wondering how we work the washing machines. Do we need tokens?"

"No, just a couple of Loonies."

Laughing, *"I've got one loonie back in the tent!"* thinking of Mike.

To say she wasn't amused would be an understatement. *Oh shit, is she actually being serious...a loonie....what the hell is that?*

"*I'm probably being a bit daft, but what is a loonie?*" I almost pleaded.

Looking ever so slightly smug, Ms Frosty explained, "*Mam, it's a dollar coin.*"

OK, now I'm intrigued.

"*But why is it called a Loonie?*"

"*A Loon is a sort of duck which happens to be on a dollar coin.*"

OK, got it now. A Loonie!

From Grand Prairie, we rode through the town of Dawson Creek. Mike, again, had researched the area and found out about the historic Kiskatinaw Bridge. Taking a turn just after the village of Farmington, we discovered the historic timber bridge which curves nine degrees along its 162.5 metres (534 feet) length. That's the technical stuff and Mike being an ex Engineer, was 'lost' in the creation of the bridge, the how's and the why's. For me, they fascinate me in a non-technical way.

One of my favourite journeys is back home in Scotland when I cross the Forth Rail Bridge by train. The carriage is usually full to capacity with commuters and tourists. Whether they're reading, chatting or checking their mobiles; the minute we start to cross the distinctive red coloured Rail Bridge, silence descends and faces turn to gaze in awe out of the window. Is it the view down across the Firth of Forth, or is it the bridge itself that mesmerizes people?

As soon as we reach the other side, the spell is broken and passengers go back to what they were doing before the crossing. Sometimes the best view of a bridge is from a distance and that's what we did after crossing the Kiskatinaw Bridge. Riding further on, we found an ideal spot to stop and look back at the curved timber bridge which almost appeared to 'grow' out of the surrounding landscape.

The day had been an enjoyable journey without thinking

of where we would be staying that night. We have a destination which is still Alaska but the journey is as important, if not more so. A pilgrimage of discovery; what will we see or experience along the way? A journey of self-discovery at the same time; I'm discovering me.

Riding into the small town of Fort St John, we noticed that the town was bustling with fire fighters. Having seen the recent news reports about the wildfires raging across Alberta, I guessed that this had to be the reason for so many firefighters being in a small town like Fort St John. And, sure enough, as we left the town the following morning, the land on either side of us was blackened and burnt. Although the fire in this area was out, the acrid smell still lingered in the air.

Further on our journey, we heard reports of the fire heading back towards Fort St John and the townsfolk were being evacuated. A battle still not won.

Lynn Aitken

The North American Bald Eagle.

Daddy
Buffalo

The grass and flowers
prove so much sweeter
      than us!

I'm intrigued! Buckinghorse River, Jackfish Creek and Pink Mountain. Heading towards Fort Nelson, we rode by these curiously named places/towns, all the while mulling over how they came about. Is Jackfish a type of fish or was it a person?

The campsite on the edge of Fort Nelson was open and quite quiet, enabling us to choose where we set up the tent. Looking at the lush green grass that was the obvious spot, where else?

The Messerschmitt size mosquitoes were obviously delighted that we chose to camp on their territory where they had been waiting in anticipation for the first of the happy campers to come along!! And on the menu this week was good Scottish blood!! We're both Scottish but Mike's blood tastes much nicer than mine! Or so the skeeters had decided and I was absolutely fine with that.

During the night, I woke to the sound of geese flying overhead. It was also 'nature calling' time for me, so dragging myself out of the warmth of my sleeping bag, I ventured outside. Looking up, the flock of geese appeared ghostly in the moonlight.

I'm glad I went out at that time and also that we weren't in a hotel room this night as, above us, the skies were moving. The Aurora Borealis, or Northern Lights, swayed and danced across the sky with different shades of green.

This was Mother Nature's light show. Who needs fireworks? Seeing the Northern Lights was also a sign that we were now, well and truly, in the northern hemisphere. The significant chill in the night air was another giveaway.

Before leaving Fort Nelson, a lady had told us about the *cloud iridescence* that are sometimes seen in the northern skies. *Rainbow clouds* she called them and best seen with sunglasses on. I've certainly seen rainbows and we see plenty of clouds in Scotland, but rainbow clouds?

I was intrigued, but not really thinking that we would see this phenomenon, we rode away from Fort Nelson. Noticing some clouds floating above us in the skies, I lowered my sun visor and there they were ...rainbow clouds or clouds iridescence. I remember, as a child, having a bottle of soapy suds and a bubble wand, the aim to blow the biggest bubble without it popping.

It leaves the bubble wand and floats through the air with the colours of the spectrum shimmering over the surface of the bubble. These were the colours in the rainbow clouds. To this day, whenever the sun is shining through the clouds, I quite often pop my sunglasses on and gaze up hoping that I would see the rainbow clouds again, but I never have.

The roads from Fort Nelson going northwest are far better than the long, straight and tedious ones further south. The highway becoming more interesting and scenic, and ever so slightly bendy, but still nothing like the twisties we're used to in Scotland.

After a day in the saddle, the thought of relaxing in the soothing thermal waters of the Liard Hot Springs was tantalizing. No sooner had we set up camp, than we were in our swimming kit and walking along the wooden boardwalk over a warm, water swamp through a boreal forest towards the springs. The steam rising from the swamp was eerie and haunting. This is where moose and other wildlife come to feed on the lush plant life which thrives as a result of the warmth of the springs.

I was naive to believe that we would have the springs to ourselves. The campsite wasn't too busy but I sort of hoped that, at this time of year, it would be quieter, a wilderness. *Are there any real wildernesses left in the world,* I wonder?

I don't know why, but whenever I see hot springs, there's a part of me that thinks the water's going to be disappointingly tepid. I'm always pleasantly surprised when I wade in and the water is bath temperature and almost boiling where it surfaces from underground. Hot springs are, undoubtedly, amazing natural wonders of the world. Soaking in the steamy, whiffy waters, I could feel my muscles slowly relax. I don't mind if I smell slightly of rotten eggs, it's worth it!

Sitting by the fire later that evening, Mike offered me a vanilla spiced whisky. Now, I'm a wine gal and never (normally) drink whisky.

Two whiskies later, (yes, I know I'm a lightweight!), I was feeling a bit tipsy.

"*Right, time to hit the sack?*" Mike suggested.

"*OK, sounds good, but we'd better put the fire out*', I replied, followed by, '*I'll do it!*"

Have I mentioned, yet, about my SHEWEE?

- A Shewee - a portable female urinating device - aka, liberating!

If a man can extinguish a fire by peeing on it, then so could I! Feeling empowered, using my SHEWEE and giggling, I successfully doused the fire! If there were any bears wandering around in the forest, I'm sure they would be staying well clear of this mad human lady who could pee standing up!

I slept so well that night and woke up feeling wonderful; no hangover. I think I could get used to vanilla spiced whisky.

Before breakfast, I went for my usual walk, a bit of exercise before a day on the bikes.

Mike was already up and heading back to the springs for a final dip in the waters.

I didn't see any moose at the swamp, however heading out of the campsite, I caught sight of a herd of buffalo with their babies. Not taking any chances as mums are very protective over their young and these are massive beasts, I stood still, watching and photographing the herd walking in a line across my path a hundred metres ahead. One baby, inquisitive of me, looked in my direction. I don't know whether mummy buffalo was grunting at me or telling baby buffalo off, but I looked around for an escape route! Baby buffalo listened to his mum and they continued on their way, probably to their daytime feeding ground.

The wildlife we were seeing along the Alcan was quite incredible. Black bears, a couple of grizzly, coyote, mountain goats, porcupine and amazingly, a wolverine. These elusive animals are extremely shy and I didn't think we would be lucky enough to catch sight of one. So, when I saw a wolverine grazing at the side of the road, I was gobsmacked. Mike missed it and, to be honest, I only caught a fleeting sight of it, but I saw it all the same.

From British Columbia, we entered the Yukon. We were now losing track of how many black bears we were seeing. Always respectful, we kept our distance but on one occasion stopping to watch a black bear up on the ridge above us, I took the opportunity to scoff an energy bar, you know the fruity ones? Mike was busy with the camera trying to take a video. I was mid snack bar, when I saw the bear stop eating the vegetation and sniff the air.

Oh shit, I thought, *it can smell my snack bar!* Duh!!

I quickly put the snack bar back into my top box and hopefully the smell disappeared as I closed the lid. Thankfully the bear went back to grazing but it was time to go before he changed his mind.

Mile 635 of the Alaska Highway and we rode into the town of Watson Lake, home to the largest collection of stolen road signs in the world.

In 1942, before Watson Lake existed, there was a military airbase here. Private Carl K. Lindley, a young soldier, was ordered to repair the directional post.

Whilst carrying out his task, Carl was a bit homesick, so decided to add a sign of his own pointing towards his hometown, Danville, Illinois. Little did Carl know that his homesickness brought about the creation of *Signpost Forest* which now has over 72,000 Signs from all four corners of the earth. I wonder if Almondbank, our village, would miss its sign?

Signpost Forest is a rather quirky but fascinating place to wander around and all because a young lad was longing for home. I wonder if the residents embrace the influx of tourists wanting to see the myriad of placards and all that brings about.

Odd sign, but strangely understood once you
have ridden over the bridge ahead!

WHITEHORSE; CAPITAL CITY OF THE YUKON

How could I ever have imagined that I would visit places such as Whitehorse? I had only ever heard of these faraway, frontier towns in books and on television. It was prospectors who flocked here in search of gold, not people like me; little Lynn from Scotland on her motorcycle.

Although being the capital of the Yukon, Whitehorse isn't a big town. That said, there's vibrancy here, an energy; Whitehorse has a happy ambience about it. I immediately took to The Wilderness City. Could I live here though? No, I don't think so. There's a reason it's known as The Wilderness City! Whitehorse is a 'city' in the middle of the wilderness, a beautiful wilderness but a wilderness all the same. I feel at home in the countryside; the peace and being surrounded by nature is my relaxation. I never feel lonely out walking through the woods and, at the same time, I enjoy the occasional shopping trip into town. But a place like Whitehorse is just too remote and isolated for me.

The campsite in Whitehorse was pretty basic but it had the advantage of being on the banks of the Yukon just outside Whitehorse itself. Once the tent was up, we took a leisurely stroll along the river path heading into town.

Mike saw the Bald Eagle first, soaring above the river on the thermals. Easily identifiable with its white head, we watched the strong, majestic bird catch a fish and then land onto a sandbank to eat it, all the while keeping an eye on anything that could steal the fish from him/her! Too far really to take a good photo, we stood still, spellbound, watching this owner of the skies.

Walking around Whitehorse, we soon realised that the majority of the townsfolk are Native Americans or First Nation. Their history and how Whitehorse came about is well documented in the museum. Before the gold rush, the First Nation communities would have thrived here in the same way they had for centuries, hunting buffalo, fishing in the mighty Yukon and raising their families. The discovery of gold by Skookum Jim and George Carmack on 16th August, 1896, changed all of that and so began the Klondike Gold Rush.

A loud pop through the night and I found myself being pushed over to one side of my mattress. One of the seams on my Exped mattress had popped open and the air was no longer divided evenly. At first, I was annoyed as this was an expensive piece of equipment and vital to ensuring a good night's sleep. However, with expensive kit, there's usually a guarantee that you'll get a replacement or something can be repaired. That guarantee would be as good as useless if we had been a distance from a town. As it was, Whitehorse relies on outdoor type shops and we soon found a top-notch camping store.

The mattress had been bought in the UK so the Whitehorse shop was under no obligation to exchange it, but they were also suppliers of Exped and that was good enough for them to offer us a replacement mattress. Unfortunately, the shop only stocked the synthetic mattresses rather than the more expensive down which we had. No matter, we thought, we'll just make do with that one, or rather, I would! It actually turned out that the cheaper synthetic Exped was just as comfortable as the down and, better still, easier to deflate and roll up when moving on. Score!

On that day, riding around Whitehorse, we met a family with a grandmother in tow. They were in Whitehorse having a trip down memory lane. The elderly grandmother once lived there and the family were treating her to this holiday.

"Yes, dear, I used to live here with my husband," she informed me.

How lovely this dear little lady was, I thought.

"Oh, it's all coming back to me, the walk over the Chilkoot Pass when I was 73 years old."

Eh? Taking another look at this fragile wee soul, *did I hear that right?*, I thought!

"Excuse me. Did you just say that you walked the Chilkoot Pass at 73 years old?" I asked, astonished.

"Yes, my dear. It was tough, but I did it!" she replied,

"I was a champion gold panner," she continued, *"my daddy taught me how to pan for gold. The Chilkoot Pass was part of the gold rush history, so I just decided that I would walk it."*

The Chilkoot Pass, a 33 mile hike, acquired fame during the Klondike gold rush. Hiking through a diverse landscape, from coastal rainforest, up to the dizzy heights and through dry forest, the stampeders went in search of the golden dream. I wonder how many found their chunk of wealth. Sometimes we meet people in life who stop us in our tracks and this little old lady was one of them. She was truly amazing and quite clearly not ready to put her feet up and grow old.

That's going to be me, I thought. I keep telling our bambinos that I'm not going to be a wee old biddy who's happy sitting at home watching soaps on TV, waiting for my family to visit. I'll be the one visiting them and, hopefully on my motorbike! I'm going to go out with a bang! Hell, maybe I'll walk the Chilkoot Trail when I'm 73!

From Whitehorse, we took a day's ride to Carcross, previously called Caribou Crossing. I prefer Caribou Crossing but the name was changed in 1902 to Carcross as there are other 'Caribou Crossing' settlements in British Columbia and Alaska.

Situated on the shores of Lake Bennett, the small settlement today is quite idyllic and quaint with colourful wooden buildings and totem poles. The aroma of freshly baked biscuits and bread wafted from one of the buildings, enticing us in. The smell of baking conjured up fond memories of the bakeries in Germany we shopped in each day, and sure enough, this bakery in Carcross was run by a German lady!

The Carcross of today gives a 'nod' to both the First Nation and their culture and to the history of the thousands of prospectors all with dreams of striking it rich.

Not just totem poles and freshly baked sourdough bread, Carcross has a desert! Yes, you read that right, a desert; and not the hot and dry variety. Just north of the town, Carcross Desert is known as the smallest desert in the world, just 640 acres. In actual fact, the 'desert' is actually the remains of an ancient, glacial lake. Stepping onto the sand, I almost expected a desert warmth to suddenly wash over me, but nope, same temperature as a minute ago. The desert would be quite something during the winter covered in snow. With that thought, it leads me to wonder if a genuine desert would ever experience snow?

Yes, is the answer to that question. In February 2019, we went back to the Sonoran desert to visit Kathy and Jim and it snowed! Seeing all the Saguaro Cacti with their 'caps' of snow on them, was incredible.

Auf Wiedersehen, Whitehorse. I like the German way of saying goodbye; quite literally meaning, until we meet again. Little did we know.

Nestled at the foot of the St Elias Mountain Range and the gateway to Kluane National Park, Haines Junction is at a junction! Connecting the coastal town of Haines in Alaska to the Alaska Highway, the small welcoming community has a charm of its own, and an amazing cafe/bakery! It's strange that I quite often associate places either by food or people!

Leaving Haines Junction the following morning, the air felt cold and damp upon my skin, the Mexican heat was like a distant memory. Looking up at the mountains, wisps of clouds drifted between the trees.

The ride to Beaver Creek would take just under four hours, however, after an hour, I could feel the cold creeping through me. Mike had mentioned that we would stop for lunch at Destruction Bay, so this thought kept me going.

At times like this, I try to keep my mind occupied so that

I'm not just thinking about the cold, although, I have to say that this time my mind kept drifting back to my body bracing itself against the icy chill.

What was I thinking about? The name, 'Destruction Bay'. We're back to names! *How on earth did it get its name*? I would have to find out when we got there, but my guess is that some significant event had happened there.

The wind was howling as we reached Destruction Bay and I had a feeling that this might be a clue to the origin of the name. Warming up in the motel/restaurant/gas station/shop, I discovered that, in the 1940's, a newly built construction camp was almost destroyed during a storm, so hence the name!

Historical mile 1202 of the Alaska Highway, Beaver Creek is just 20 miles from U.S./Canada border and gateway to Alaska. Alaska!!! This is true frontier land and we were ready to explore as the pioneers had before us, although we were on motorbikes rather than horses! So, OK, maybe not quite the same, nevertheless an achievement all the same.

Beaver Creek is not only famous for being a border town for entering or leaving Alaska, but also home to Buckshot Betty. A restaurant owner with cabins and a fellow biker, Betty gave us the best cabin for half the price. Luxury!

Small in stature with a big personality, Betty is quite a character in town and will happily tell you the story of how she out rode a grizzly running alongside her.

Still worrying about Hazel, we often video called her and after logging onto the internet at Buckshot Betty's, we were soon chatting to our little girl.

This was the moment Mike and I knew that we just wanted to go home. Hazel needed us and had for a long time but had kept it from us so as not to ruin our trip. Ruin our trip? This adventure was nothing compared to our family. We closed the laptop, looked at each other, both knowing what we were going to do.

"*Time to go home,*" Mike said, tears welling up in his eyes.

The tears weren't because we were heading home, no, they were for Hazel.

"*Absolutely Mike,*" I replied, already crying. While I'm writing this, tears are welling up all over again. *Breathe Lynn, take a moment.*

Ok, I'm back.

Being Friday evening, the travel company would be closed for the weekend. All we could do was email them asking for our flights to be brought forward to ASAP. It was 2000 miles to Vancouver where we could fly from, so early start the next morning and ride as much as we could each day just to eat up the miles and get home to Hazel.

And that's what we did. First, before leaving Beaver Creek, we contacted Hazel and told her our decision; we were coming home.

"*No mum, you're not!*" she cried.

"*Yes we are, we want to and need to*"

"*But Alaska. You have to keep going and go to Alaska. Please, I'm begging you,*"

There are times in life that wee white lies are totally OK and this was one of them.

"*We've been,*" I lied "*we rode over the border this morning; it's only 20 miles away. We made it, Hazel, to Alaska, we did it and now, we're coming home*"

Hazel was still not happy but resigned and she also looked relieved.

So, with Alaska just up the road, we turned around. Alaska will always be there and we'll be back.

STEWART-CASSIAR HIGHWAY

We rode all day to Whitehorse, 400 miles eaten up with 60 miles of it being un-surfaced and dusty! The dust was made worse by trucks driving along the road. Mike was in front as usual but regularly disappeared in a cloud of dust.

The decision was made to stay in hotels until we reached the campsite in Vancouver, allowing us to just get up each morning and head southwards, hoping that the freight company could get us home as quickly as possible. We also wanted to be able to get internet access to contact Hazel at each stop-over.

Although I had lied to Hazel that we made it to Alaska, we could tell her when we got home that we actually did. Yes, we turned back within 20 miles of the border, but we could still enter into Alaska whilst heading towards Vancouver.

Taking the Cassiar Highway, we turned onto the 37A towards Stewart which is in British Columbia, but 3 Kms from there is Hyder, a small town in Alaska. And that's what we did, so we made it to Alaska, albeit a different route. Hyder itself is tiny and, at this time of year, was pretty much closed. Photo shoot in Alaska and back into Canada for an overnight stopover in Stewart.

Leaving Stewart the next morning, we passed so many black bear grazing at the side of the road that we lost count! Another spectacular sight was a blue coloured glacier suspended in its frozen state.

Stopping our bikes to enjoy nature's marvel, we both vowed that we would return to this stunning land.

Taking the Stewart-Cassiar Highway, folk warned us that it was narrow, winding and the surface not great. Wrong! The highway is more akin to our roads back home, making it a nice change from the long, straight roads we had been riding on.

Eventually, we were leaving the beautiful countryside behind and Vancouver was looming ever nearer. The greenery grew increasingly sparser, replaced by buildings and more people. As for Vancouver, my appetite for sightseeing was gone and I saw Vancouver as a place to fly out from to get home to my family. Time to go home.

What can I say about the ride from Stewart to Vancouver? I remember the names of the places we stayed overnight, but that's all. I don't want to do these an injustice by not mentioning them. So, Smithers, Prince George and Clinton; we thank you for giving us a place to eat and to lay our heads. And maybe we'll be back one day and check out your towns.

One of the towns we passed through was Houston, British Columbia. Riding along past Houston, I couldn't help but think it surreal, that we started this journey in Houston, Texas, and we were now passing another Houston, almost at the end of the trip. Apart from admiring the scenery as we're riding along, there's also a lot of time to think and reflect, hence the comparison between the two Houstons.

Another sign along Highway 16 was a warning to women not to hitchhike. It's nicknamed the 'Highway of Tears'. The highway is renowned for women disappearing, officially 18 but the numbers are supposed to exceed 40! Researching further into this, I also discovered that a lot of the women were First Nation. I used to hitchhike with a friend when I was in my teens and if, I saw a sign warning us not to, I would have heeded it, so I'm hoping that the sign has maybe saved lives. Now, thinking back to my hitchhiking days, my friend, Arlene and I had a plan.

The one who sat in the back of the car had the rucksack

with the cooking pans hanging on the outside of it so, if the driver threatened us, the person in the back could bop him on the head with the pan! What numpties we were! The person who would have been threatening us, was also in charge of a vehicle that we were in, travelling at X speed along the road!! Luckily, we didn't have to bop anyone on the head!! However, we did find ourselves in tricky situations and were lucky to be travelling as a pair rather than alone.

As we approached Vancouver and civilisation, I was relieved; not because of the miles we had travelled and the sore bottom; I was relieved because we would soon be home, back with Hazel.

There was a part of me, though, that was sad to leave the wildlife, but, in a way, I'm glad I felt sad, as I knew, then, that we would be back. I didn't know when, but I knew we would. The wildlife, for me, has been the highlight of the adventure. I love Scotland and, in all our travels, I haven't found a place as stunningly beautiful and haunting as my homeland. However, where in Scotland would I come across bears and moose? We have our deer and our hairy highland cattle, but bears?

We had made good time in reaching Vancouver and arrived at the campsite on the Thursday which meant that we would be able to see a bit of Vancouver before dropping the bikes off at the airfreight depot on the Saturday. The flights were still booked for the coming Tuesday. Almost there!

We had heard of the Capilano Suspension Bridge, a popular tourist attraction in Vancouver 70 metres above the Capilano River, the bridge was built in 1889 by a Scottish land developer, George Grant MacKay. Us Scots get everywhere! The bridge was originally made from hemp rope, however replaced in 1903 with a wire cable bridge.

We paid our money and joined a queue of people all wanting to go over the bridge. We shuffled slowly over and then we shuffled up over smaller bridges through the treetops. There's no doubt that it's an amazingly beautiful place looking down over the unique rainforest, but it's crazily busy with tourists, us included! Shuffling along in the tightly packed crowd of people, I suddenly felt claustrophobic! My instincts were to get out of there as quickly as possible and yet, I could hardly move; I was almost being 'carried' along.

Normally I'm alright in situations like this, but we've been in really remote places and I was just feeling the effects of being amongst people again. Taking a deep breath, I composed myself, and continued shuffling along!

The bikes were to be as spotless as possible so that there was no chance of taking any bugs or bacteria etc back to the UK. That's fine, we thought. We would ride to a garage with a power hose. Arriving at the first garage we found, we noticed a queue of cars waiting to be cleaned. Joining the queue, the lady in front of us looked quizzically at our bikes.

"Are you waiting to clean the bikes?" she asked.

"Yes, they're filthy and we need them spotless before they travel."

"So, how are you going to take them through the carwash?"

Before answering, I looked ahead and, sure enough, it was a drive through car wash! She must have thought we had some magic way of going through it! Or, just maybe, she thought that we were stupid, which, yes, I admit, we were!

"Oops, I didn't see that it was a drive through!" I admitted.

Off we rode in search of another place to clean the bikes. We must have ridden around for an hour or so and found nothing. All we could do was to head back to the campsite and ask there if they knew of somewhere.

Again, we were humbled by the kindness of folk on our travels. The campsite office printed off the paperwork we needed and lent us a high powered hose and soapy water to clean the bikes in preparation for flying.

This time flying, the bikes had to be completely empty of kit, so we bought a couple of empty holdalls for our luggage, including tent etc.

After dropping our clean bikes off at the airfreight depot, we took a taxi to a hotel, our home for the last three nights in

Vancouver.

A few people we have met on the trip and, also, when we got back home, asked us the same question, *"Did you take anything you didn't need or, not take something that you had to buy over there?"*

To be honest, the first time we were asked this question, I really had to think. I've included our kit list for the trip in the book which Mike had put together over the months leading up to leaving. We had watched programmes such as 'Horizons Unlimited' and Mike even attended one of their rallies to gain information and chat to other bikers who had undertaken trips like this. Soaking up all the hints and tips given to us, I believe, helped our own adventure. I have lost track of the adventure books written by other bikers that Mike had read before we left.

So, to answer that question.......no, not really. We took the right amount of kit and, more importantly, the right type of kit. Perhaps, with hindsight, we would have bought synthetic rather than down mattresses; or left out the extra fuel bladders, but we weren't to know and we may well have needed them; who knows?

"What about the axe we had to buy?" Mike's just reminded me.

I had forgotten all about that, possibly because Mike was, for the most part, *he who makes the fire*! So, yes, something we did have to buy was an axe. Most of the campsites we stayed in had fire pits, many of which had free firewood.

To start a fire, we needed kindling (small pieces of wood) and so, we needed an axe.

We, or should I say, Mike, was well prepared for our adventure of a lifetime. Going back to that question people asked of us; I know something I didn't take with me, and that was confidence.

I still, to this day, doubt myself, but I came back from the trip with a lot more confidence than I left with and knowing that you can be gazing in awe over something as wondrous as the vast Grand Canyon, but I'm happiest when I'm with my family.

In Vancouver, all I wanted was to get home as soon as possible. I needed to be with my family. But, we're coming back; back to Canada and Alaska and maybe into the Arctic Circle. Another adventure awaits Mike and I.

Who would believe it? Our UK registered bikes had been accepted smoothly and efficiently in all the countries we had ridden through, that was until we tried to 'import' them back into the UK!

Touching down in a wet and windy Glasgow at 7 am in the morning, we took ourselves off to collect our bikes. Our biggest worry was that the bikes hadn't been put on the plane, but, yes, they were.

The bikes were off the plane and just waiting for Customs to put their stamp of approval on the paperwork. Then, we were good to go. How difficult could it be? We had all the correct paperwork but still Customs took until 3 pm to release the bikes.

Mike, at one point, even had his hands on his bike when he was asked if he could help take his bike off the pallet!

Mike had catnapped on the plane but I hadn't slept at all, so I was starting to feel the effects of the journey back across the Atlantic.

Trying to sleep on airport chairs is nigh on impossible, but we still tried! Oh to stretch out in a comfy bed. That day we got to know Glasgow airport quite well and I always like to see positives in situations. Whilst waiting for the bikes, we discovered a food van in the airport grounds but away from all the people who were commuting.

We happened upon it by chance and, for me, that was the positive in having to wait for most of the day. The food van was where the airport staff went to rather than expensive airport chains.

Delicious homemade food at a decent price. My mouth's watering thinking back to the scrambled egg roll I enjoyed from the van and a proper cup of tea!

Eventually our bikes were cleared through Customs, but now we had to load our kit back onto them. By the time the bikes were ready for the off, the weather had worsened and the rain was no longer vertical! Heading out, bracing ourselves against the wind, we rode straight into the Glasgow rush hour.

Hazel was so near and yet, every minute crawling through the traffic, felt like an eternity.

The feeling when we arrived at Hazel's flat in Stirling and the three of us hugging is beyond describing. They say that home is where the heart is and, for us, it's where our family is. We are Lynn and Mike who went on an adventure, but we are also, mum and dad and Nanny Lynn and Pop Pops.

Now we were on another journey, this one right by Hazel's side. This journey is a tough one though! For any parent to watch their child go through the heartache that Hazel was going through is harrowing. I am in awe of Hazel and her inner strength, a strength that will see her through this.

She did see it through. And, it was tough. The times we've just had to hug her, be there for her. Then there was Hazel going off travelling to Vietnam and Thailand, losing her passport and all her belongings and having to come home. But, that's a whole other story!

Hazel's now a primary school teacher and loving it. She's also found happiness and love with Tom, who is also part of our family.

And what happened to the bastard who attacked her? Well, his life 'stopped' that night because he's serving an eight year and nine month prison sentence.

DESTINATION; ALASKA

Where have the last two years gone? Has it really been that long since our last jaunt over the other side of the 'pond'? It was always the plan to go back someday and finish the trip; that time is now, summer of 2018.

For nearly a year, Mike has been planning the route, sorting the flights, checking the *Milepost* magazine etc etc. As well as the planning, our television seems to be permanently tuned to programmes such as *Life Below Zero* and *Building Alaska!* It's a strange thing that any house we visit, their television seems to default to Alaska focused programmes! If the end of the world was nigh, I'm sure our family would be well equipped with the survival skills they would need! Even my mother-in-law now knows how to build a shelter or make a fire without mod cons! Our oldest son, Vaughan, is a prepper! He's preparing for the end of civilisation, as we know it, which involves having a *Doomsday Cupboard!*

We had also done the maths and realised that it would be marginally cheaper to hire bikes over in Anchorage rather than ship our own over there. Both of us would have preferred to ride our own bikes but it proved too costly. If a trip is longer than four weeks, then, it seems that it pays to ship the bikes however; we were going for just under four weeks. Not only the cost but also the fact that we could fly our bikes into Anchorage and yet, not out of there. I'm not sure why this is but we didn't have the time to head back down to Vancouver on this trip. So, rentals it would have to be. Mike was renting a V Strom and mine, the same as I have at home, a lowered F700GS. To me, it felt like we were going on an adventure without part of our 'team'. Our bikes would be tucked up in the garage waiting for us when we got home.

Running up to leaving for Anchorage, it suddenly felt like ground rush. One minute we were saying *'next year'* and before we knew it, it was, *'this year'* and then *'next month'*.

I loved watching Mike pour over the map, planning fuel stops and where to visit. I just hoped that Alaska was going to be all he hoped it would be. For as long as I can remember, Mike's hankered after visiting the last frontier.

With the trip organised and almost upon us, we managed to travel the length and breadth of the UK to see the family.

I have this 'thing'. I have to see my family before leaving on an adventure.

Mike sighs and says to the kids, *"Mum has to see you all just in case she dies."*

I know we're not going to die, not yet anyway. In fact, I'm not planning on going anywhere for a long time, apart from the Yukon and Alaska that is!

I'm back working at Scone Palace selling entry tickets to visitors from all over the world and the occasional stint at guiding. My job is great and I work with an amazing team of people. I realised that I would be taking a month off right at the start of the really busy time of the season, but the management have known about the trip, part 2, for the last year and were happy to give me the time off.

Feeling slightly guilty that I was leaving the ticket team one person down, I worked right up until two days before we flew. So, in between working, we managed to squeeze in going to Brize Norton to see Vaughan and Lacey, driving up to the top of mainland Scotland to Thurso to see Daryl, Kim and wee Dharyl, and moving Hazel back from Hamilton after her University course had finished! Hazel and her boyfriend, Tom, were looking after our dog, Brodie and the house which was a great help. Then there were the parents in Edinburgh. I still feel awful that I didn't get to see my auntie Nancy but, at 92 years old, she's got such a hectic social life, I knew that her diary is fuller than ours!

Now, where was I? The family. Daryl, our middle son announced last year that they were expecting another baby. What wonderful news and the fact that Kim's due date was the 7th July 2018, we would be back by then. We could get back, jump in the car and head north to look after wee Dharyl when Kim had to go to hospital. Sorted.

"*Mum, Dad,*" Daryl said. "*We have a problem. The baby's now due earlier on the 25th June and you'll still be in Alaska.*"

Mike, pouring himself a beer, answered, "*Daryl, **we** don't have a problem. **You** have a problem. We'll be in Alaska.*"

Sometimes it's good to not have too much time to dwell on leaving and a trip like this, and we were definitely *last minute dot com!*

The morning of our departure was here and I was still making lists for Hazel and Tom. Writing lists always makes me feel calmer, as once down on paper, it's one thing less to worry about. I'm not sure if handing over my extensive lists calmed Tom and Hazel down at all! They probably waited until we left and did their own thing.

Surprisingly, I slept well the night before we headed off; it was either because I was shattered from the run up to going, or, my head was at peace as a result of my list writing!

Waking up early, I felt ready for adventure part 2, but first, take Brodie for a walk in the woods. Although it was still early in the morning, the sun was warm; it was going to heat up quite nicely today. *Water the plants!* Another item for the list!

Watching my furry friend run across the field and through the kissing gate into the woods, I wonder what goes on in Brodie's head. Does he sense that we're leaving for a while? Taking off after a deer, no, he's in *normal mode*. A quick blast of the whistle, and he came bounding back to me, tongue hanging out, happy with his lot.

It's Sod's law if I'm trying to keep clothes clean, that's when I'll manage to get them dirty, and that morning was one of those moments! Tripping over a tree root, I fell onto the only muddy part of the path. Brodie didn't bat an eyelid as it's a regular thing for me to hit the deck! But, why did it have to happen on the day we were leaving?

Shit, what am I going to do? I know, I'll get home, rinse the knees of my trousers and pop them for a few minutes in the tumble dryer.

Trousers cleaned, we said our goodbyes to Hazel, Tom and Brodie and left Almondbank in the car, heading to Glasgow Airport.

An hour into the journey, I checked, yet again, that I had my passport. *Passport; check. Purse; check. Cards; check. Driving license, oh SHIT!!!! It's here, it's here, I know it is. Oh my giddy aunt, it's in the other purse!*

I must have said, "*Oh shit*" out loud because Mike looked across at me saying, "*What?*" Now, this wasn't just a "*what?*" as in "*what's the weather like, what?*"

This was a "*What the fuck are you just about to tell me you've forgotten?*"

"*I'm so sorry Mike; I've left my driving license in my other purse.*"

"*We're screwed!!*" he yelled at me.

"*Oh, shit! I'm so so sorry. I know; we'll ask Hazel to post it to Anchorage. We can get it when we get there.*"

My thinking was that we were in Anchorage for three days before we picked up our rental bikes.

Mike, however, wasn't on my wavelength, which is probably a good thing, for him!

"*What??*" he shouted, looking at me as if I had finally lost the plot!

"*Take my phone, phone Hazel, ask her to find your license, call a taxi to pick it up and drive it straight to meet us at the airport.*"

Even when Mike's stressed, he can still remain quite logical!

While Mike concentrated on driving us to the airport, I frantically called Hazel, hoping that she had her phone with her. She did! Hazel took charge of the situation and, thankfully, managed to get a taxi to us along with the driving license.

What an expensive and stressful start to the trip. £100 taxi fare, one retrieved driving license and my husband having an anxiety meltdown. I'm not joking when I say that I was checking where the heart defibrillator stations were!

Panic over and Mike's blood pressure better after a beer, we took off from Glasgow heading for a transfer in Iceland. Going back to Mike's blood pressure, am I driving him to drink?

Checking in at Departures, we realised that we were sitting rows away from each other. Now, you may be thinking that, after the driving license incident, this would've been quite a good idea; but Mike actually wanted to sit beside me! How sweet is that?

The flight attendant could see us far enough, her expression said it all; we were problem passengers. But, we stood our ground and were allowed to sit beside each other, and better still, our seats were right by the toilets!

The first stage of our journey took us to Iceland, the land of fire and ice, where we transferred to the flight to Anchorage. At the next departure gate, I glanced around at our fellow passengers, and immediately knew that this could only be the Alaska flight and not bound for Ibiza. The guy dressed in brown denim dungarees looking like Grizzly Adams proved the point.

Anchorage was in sight and looking out of the plane window, the jagged, snow capped mountains were welcoming us. We were actually in Alaska!

On leaving the airport, although sunny, the chill in the air seemed to come straight from the snowy mountains. Summer is but a short season here in Alaska.

We had made a last minute decision to stay the first night in a cheap and cheerful hotel. Cheapish it was, but cheerful it wasn't. A bored looking receptionist checked us into the 'sterile' room. Hey ho, it was for one night only, a place to lay our heads.

The rest of the trip, apart from one other night, would be camping. Not only do we love camping, it also helped eke out the money.

Although it was early evening in Alaska, this was now the middle of the night to us and, although having had no sleep since Scotland, we were still wide awake, no sign of jet lag and hungry. Apparently jet lag is the change in our circadian rhythms, whatever that is. If jet lag is an actual physical thing, why don't pilots and aircrew suffer from this? Maybe it's something they just get used to as part and parcel of the job. The only feeling I've ever noticed after flying to a different time zone is drained, but not tired as in 'sleepy'.

Refreshed after a good night's sleep, the next morning, we checked out of the hotel and headed to the free campsite at the back of the Harley Davidson and Motoquest dealers. A small patch of grass, but more welcoming than a bland hotel room. There was even a toilet and shower facility; luxury.

As ever, once our tent was pitched, I felt more at home and safe in a foreign country. It's a safe haven to me, somewhere familiar. It might sound weird, but it works for me.

It's strange and expensive having to rely on taxis to get around and we were without our rental bikes for another couple of days. Where we were camping was on the outskirts of town and so, too far to walk anywhere really. Mike came up with the solution: rent a couple of bicycles, and that's just what we did. Cycling seemed to be quite popular here in Anchorage which I was surprised about, as any other American town/city we'd visited previously, I can't remember seeing anyone on bicycles. Finding a bicycle rental shop in downtown Anchorage was quite easy, the fact that there were a row of bicycles outside the shop was a fairly good clue! We weren't the only folk looking for rentals; *I hope they don't run out of bikes!*

It wasn't long before we were being fitted for our bikes and there were still plenty to choose from. Straddling my, soon to be, mode of transport; my feet were on tiptoes.

"*I'll lower that seat for you*" said the guy, fetching a spanner.

"*Do you think I'm a short arse?*" I said, laughing.

"That is so cute how you say that," he laughed, *"we say 'ass' but the way you say 'arse' is great. That's made my day. For that, I'll give you three extra hours with the bikes free,"* he continued.

Hmmm, note to self; they like my Scottish accent. This may just come in handy!

Cycling back to the campsite confirmed that Anchorage was a cycle friendly town as there were plenty designated paths and drivers seemed to be mindful of cyclists, giving us plenty of room.

It was liberating to have our own transport and, at the same time, enjoying some exercise. Since the trip of 2016, Mike's knee had worsened considerably and to walk any real distance was a struggle for him. Cycling, therefore, was the better option of getting around Anchorage.

I was enjoying the moment, cycling along, and breathing in the Alaskan air, when Mike screeched to a halt outside a shop called 'Enlighten'. Can you guess where this is going? Mike was in the military and an ex police officer, therefore an extremely law abiding man and, heaven forbid, do anything illegal. When we knew that we were coming to Alaska, he did his research and discovered that cannabis is legal in the State for medicinal and recreational use.

The shops which sell cannabis here in Alaska aren't the least bit seedy. Walking into 'Enlighten' was akin to going into a pharmacy, albeit with an overpowering 'weed' smell! Before 2016, I didn't know what cannabis smelt like.

"It smells a bit like a stock cube," Mike tried to describe it.

Now, a stock cube, I know, but I'm not sure that I would agree. The smell of cannabis is unlike any other and once you recognize the aroma, your nose tends to sense it quite easily. A smell never forgotten. Recently, in a friend's garden, I was admiring her plants. There was a strange aroma that I couldn't place.

"That smell reminds me of our trip," I said to Mike.

"Cannabis," he replied, smiling.

No, my friend isn't growing cannabis, but I now know

that there are other plants which give off a similar scent.
When our elderly friend heard what her plant smelled of, she
smiled, *"how lovely!"*

Back in 'Enlighten', the staff, friendly and professional,
seemed to know their 'stuff' and able to advise Mike which
joint, for the better word, was best for him. He walked out of
the shop, a, soon to be, chilled and happy man! Thinking back
to the driving license incident, a bit of wacky backy may have
proved helpful! But, there again, it's illegal back home and so
Mike would have been more stressed knowing that he could
have it but that would be illegal, therefore wouldn't risk it because he's a law abiding man!

Mike's proud to be a member of the British Legion and
also, the Blue Knights, a law enforcement motorcycle club.
Whenever possible he likes to meet up with members of both
fraternities. In Anchorage there was an American Legion Post,
so was keen to meet up with some of the members. I'm always
nervous meeting new people and I'm sure friends of mine will
say, *"what? No way!"* But, truth be told, I really am. I put my
smile on and hide behind my lipstick and hope that people
will see a confident lady. So, smile and lipstick on, we cycled
to the American Legion. After meeting the guys and gals, I
wondered why I'm always nervous. Again, as on our previous
trip, we met lovely, genuine folk who made us feel so welcome.

Various badges were swapped and stories of bike adven-
tures shared, along with the occasional reference to hunting
and fishing. This reminded me that we really were venturing
into the last frontier where people still hunt to survive. Although a vegetarian for most of my life, I'm cool with someone having to go out and hunt for their dinner.

The animal has enjoyed being in the wild and, hopefully,
had a good life. How many people can say that they think of
that animal when they buy their meat in the supermarket?

I do, however, have a massive issue with trapping! I
just see it as cruel and cheating and not a way that an ani-

mal should ever die. And, yet here in Alaska, there are some hunters who use this method. I will just have to avoid them or say my piece. Everyone's entitled to an opinion, say I, and this is the land of free speech, isn't it?

'I get cramps in my legs, but if I eat bananas, it goes away'

- Drunk girl in pub

Directly opposite the campsite was a traditional Alaskan Restaurant and bar. It's nice, when camping, to have somewhere in the evening to sit indoors, have a glass of wine, use the internet and people watch. Crossing the busy road, we made for Gwennies Old Alaska Restaurant.

Sitting near us in the bar was a young lass, maybe in her early twenties, obviously drunk. Drunk, loud and talking a lot of shite! From eating bananas which cures leg cramps to, possibly letting slip that her friend is making crystal meth in a lab in the valley. The drunk girl had no idea that I was listening and taking notes for my book!

One of the guys chatting to her, who also had one too many and twice her age, came up behind her and was playing keepie uppie with her boobs. Did she complain? No!

Worryingly, she staggered away to her car at just before 9 pm and drove away onto the main road. Now, if this had been the UK, we would've called the police and reported her. But this wasn't the UK and not our country. Scary though, but also 'food for thought' when riding the bikes. Not only will we be watching out for large animals running out at us, but also drunken people behind the wheel of something larger and faster than any wild animal could be. Interesting, also, that all the time we were in Anchorage, we didn't see one police car.

The Harley Davidson staff were hosting a party for bikers

to attend and included us even though we still hadn't collected our rentals. Needless to say that most of the bikes turning up were Harleys, shining chrome and all that.

Mike drew my attention to the red badge waistcoats of some of the riders. *"Can you guess who they are?"* he asked.

Looking over at the group who seemed to be acting as if they were on a higher level than anyone else, I had an inkling.

"Hell's Angels?" I answered.

"They most certainly are," Mike confirmed

"OMG, do you think that shit is going down?" I asked

Mike's reply was just to smile and shake his head.

I don't know much about the Hell's Angels other than rumours that they dabble in criminal activities and usually ride Harleys. A well known series on television was meant to depict the club. Whether any of this is true or not, intrigued, I couldn't help but occasionally glance over to the Hell's Angels at the gathering in Anchorage.

Although it was fascinating watching the goings on, I couldn't help feeling slightly out of place. We certainly didn't fit into the Harley Davidson scene. For some of the Harley riders, it seemed to be an excuse to wear designer sunglasses and not much in the way of protective motorbike kit. I turned as I heard the roar of yet another Harley riding in.

This time it was a lady rider wearing bright red lipstick, sunglasses, a tight fitting t-shirt and no helmet! This lady was making an entrance and she wasn't going to let anyone ignore her, therefore a lap of the car park was in order.

Blimey, the sun reflecting off her bike's highly polished chrome almost blinded me! I wonder if her bike ever gets dirty. Suitably noticed, she parked her bike and proceeded to high five a group of other posers, I mean bikers!

As well as beer and food, there was music, of sorts, and I can't leave out the 'Burn Out'. In the parking area above where we were camped, the 'Burn Out' was taking place. A biker revs his engine, whilst keeping the front brake locked, spinning his back wheel. Seconds later, the bike and rider disappears in a cloud of smoke, burning rubber. I stepped back, not wanting to breathe in the fumes, but no one else seemed bothered including the riders. The idea is to see whose wheel explodes and disintegrates first. I just hope they weren't planning on riding home!

After the smoke had disappeared, I was horrified to see our tent covered in tiny pieces of rubber and even more shocked to discover that the tent stank of burnt rubber! The smell soon disappeared but what the hell?

By the time we were due to leave Anchorage, we were both itching to get going on *Adventure Part 2*. We were both up bright and breezy, our tent packed up and ready to load up the bikes. I was feeling slightly anxious about riding a rental bike and it didn't help that the person in Motoquest had dreadlocks and was ever so cool.

"So, guys. You've signed all the paperwork and you know that riding a bike is dangerous," he said in a southern drawl.

No, really? Duh! Only if you're an idiot! I thought.

I looked across at Mike and knew straight away, that he was thinking exactly the same.

"So, where are you guys headed?" He continued.

After reeling off our various destinations, his eyes widened somewhat, *"sweet,"* he replied.

"So, guys. I want you to have a ride around the parking lot, just to make sure you're happy with the bikes."

Look cool, I thought!

This goes back to me not liking being watched, especially with *Mr Cool* looking on. But, we managed to convince him that, yes, we could ride a bike and he let us out on our own!

As ever, once we were on the bikes, I felt happy, relaxed and free. Riding shotgun, I could tell by Mike's body language that he was eager to see what adventure awaited us. We were off!

It wasn't long before we were leaving Anchorage city limits behind and the countryside was opening up around us.

The vastness was staggering, an endless expanse of wilderness. And yet a wilderness smacks of nothingness, an uninhabited land which isn't true of this bewitching land. Although we couldn't see any sign of life, I knew that all around us, this land was teeming with wildlife. Riding along, I bet there were eyes watching us from the bush, remaining stock still until we passed by.

We had left Anchorage bathed in sunshine; however, looking ahead in the direction we were riding, the skies were turning a slate grey heavy with rain. Up ahead and underneath the foreboding skies was Denali National Park and that was our destination. We weren't worried about the inclement weather, it was nice to be away from the topsy-turviness, we call civilization.

Further on and just outside the park boundary, we spotted a couple of cars parked at the side of the road. The occupants, out of their vehicles, looking through binoculars over the river could only mean one thing, an animal!

Parking the bikes next to the cars, Mike and I wandered over to see what the folk were looking at. Acknowledging us, the man lowered his binoculars and pointed over to the other side of the wide river.

"It's just headed back into the bush, but we think it's a moose."

Following where he was pointing, we scanned the river bank but seeing nothing, we thought we were too late. The folk all said their goodbyes, wished us a nice holiday and headed back to their cars.

I couldn't help glancing over just one last time in the hope that I would see the moose. And sure enough, there was a movement, something was coming back out of the bush and heading to the water's edge.

Mike noticed the movement at the same time and was already looking through his monocle.

"It's a wolf!" He cried excitedly.

On hearing this, the folk, almost back at their cars, came running back. Squinting, trying to focus, I started making out the shape of a lone, grey wolf. In all our previous travels, we had never managed to catch a glimpse of this noble and shy creature. But, here it was, drinking water from the river; he saw us and knew that we could see him, but that didn't seem to bother him. Did he sense that we were merely observers and no threat to him?

Mike handed me the monocle and, holding my breath, I peered through. I couldn't help gasping when I saw the wolf magnified; he seemed to be right in front of me. His stance, bold and proud as he drank from the river. He moved further along the river bank with grace and dignity and, although he was on the other side of a fairly wide river, I could see that this lone wolf was huge!

We were truly privileged to have witnessed this predator in his natural environment. Perhaps the people had seen a moose and the wolf had followed the scent down to the river. *"I wish I had my gun!"*

That broke the spell. Horrified, I turned to see who had said this; it was a man from one of the cars.

"No way! How could you?" I found myself saying out loud.

His reply was to smile and head back to the car. Looking back at the wolf, *please head back into the park Mr Wolf,* I silently pleaded. The reason; there's no hunting allowed within the National Park boundaries and there, the wolf had six million acres of safe passage and a place to call home. It was almost as if he had 'heard' my thoughts, as he turned and trotted back into the shrubbery and safety.

At that moment I knew that this was going to be an adventure filled with emotions.

DENALI; THE GREAT ONE

Denali National Park, home to the tallest mountain in North America. Denali reaches four miles up into the sky! We had seen the mountain in all its glory from the plane on approach to Anchorage and now, hopefully we'll see it in the park. I'm saying *hopefully* as although we're here and should be able to see Denali, the mountain is often shrouded in cloud. Denali was named Mount McKinley by a gold prospector in 1897, but in fact has always been known as Denali by native Alaskans. The good news is that in 1980, the mountain was officially given its original name back and so Denali, the Great One is once more.

With any of the National Parks, the first thing to do is to check in at the Visitor Centre and that's where we headed. This was to secure our tent space and to chat to the rangers who have all the information we needed to enjoy our stay. National Park visitor centres tend not to stock a lot of food, mainly basic provisions, so we always try to stock up on food before leaving town. I had also treated ourselves to a $1 wine glass each when we were in Anchorage. If I'm going to drink wine, I'd rather it was from a proper glass, albeit a budget one!

"I don't know why you're bothering," Mike declared, adding, *"They're only going to get smashed."*

"No, they're not; I'll make sure of it!" I replied. Challenge accepted, I was determined to see the trip out with two intact wine glasses!

Having found our designated tent site, we set about putting up our home for three nights; each of us had our own tasks. Looking up at the darkening skies, we were on a race against time before it rained. This felt like summer back in Scotland!

The temperature was dropping with the onset of rain, so we quickened our pace, not only to get the tent up before the rain came, but also to warm up.

The last peg in and the first drops of rain started coming down; spits and spots to begin with but we knew that there was a heavy shower on its way.

Tent up, we dived inside with our feet still sticking outside. Yanking our boots off, we zipped up the tent shutting out the rain which by now, was a downpour. I might be crazy, but one of my favourite things in life is being in a tent when it's raining.

The sound of the rain against the tent while being safe and warm inside ignites a deep down survival instinct in me. Packing up a wet tent is another matter altogether and not a pleasant one at all! But, for now, we simply embraced the moment and lay listening to the rain.

It may be summer just now but during the long winter months, Alaska is a land of snow, ice and freezing temperatures. What better way to travel from place to place than with the help of *Man's best friend,* dogs. I had heard about dog sledding or mushing, but, for some reason, to me, it seemed more of a hobby. Indeed, a sport it is, but, during the Alaskan and Northern Canadian harsh winters, it's also the most reliable way to travel.

For hundreds of years, the Inuit people have travelled in this way. Although many Alaskans and Canadians now use snowmobiles, the traditional dog sledding is still a favoured mode of transport.

Here in Denali, although no snow, we were visiting the kennels to meet the dogs who work hard throughout the winter months transporting vital supplies.

Taking the park bus, we soon arrived at the kennels and it was bitterly cold! The cold and rain couldn't dampen our spirits as we approached where the dogs were housed. Each one had their own kennel and was attached to *running circle chains*. The dogs seemed to be just as excited to see the visitors and were soon wagging their tails, barking and wanting petted. Each dog looked and acted differently from the next.

Piñata sat quietly on top of his kennel looking thoughtful, while Carpe, a Siberian looking husky, danced around eager for attention.

Gathering around to watch the demonstration, I could feel the excitement building, and it wasn't just the spectators; the dogs were eager to run.

As the sled was being prepared, the dogs started barking and howling and we knew they were saying, *"pick me, please pick me!"*

The lucky six were hooked up to the sled; each dog knew his or her own place and job within the team. The dogs who weren't chosen this time, merely settled happily back down; they would have their moment in the spotlight another time.

The dogsledder took her position, released the brake and they were off! In that moment, I realised that these dogs lived to run, and run they did. As they raced past us, the dogsledder called out to the dogs in a language alien to us.

I heard her call out the word '*haw*' and the dogs veered left.

I wonder how she gets them to stop. I thought. No sooner had this crossed my mind, when the team of dogs came back around, the dogsledder yelled '*Whoa!*' and the dogs came to a stop right in front of us. Each of the dogs was given a well deserved treat and a round of applause from us spectators. Did the dogs know that they were the stars of the show? Hell, yes!

The weather in Denali only worsened, and during the first night, it had snowed higher up in the mountains. Putting on more layers to ward off the cold, I looked up at the snowy mountain peaks. *Just like home,* I thought. Like Alaska, Scotland has unpredictable summers; we never know what to expect. June is one of those months when it's summer but spring doesn't like to let go!

And, just like back home, the only thing for it is to dress for the weather and carry on. With that in mind, we took a park bus 15 miles to Savage River. It was nice to be in the warmth, looking out at the scenery as we were driven further into the park. I kept looking out for some sign of wildlife, but it seemed that the animals may well have been sheltering from the cold and wet as well!

I call it a 'trainspotting' moment, of which I've had two in my life. What's a 'trainspotting' moment? It's from the film set in Scotland where the characters take a train ride out of the city. Getting off the train in the middle of nowhere, they were clearly not dressed for the Scottish weather or the environment and there's not a whole lot there, apart from the station platform. To say they weren't impressed was an understatement.

My first 'trainspotting' moment was up north visiting our son, Daryl and his wife, Kim. Having not long moved to Thurso, they hadn't yet visited the top of mainland Scotland, John O'Groats. For a little day trip, we took a bus to this most northerly point of the country hoping that we would have enough time to see everything before the last bus home.

We all piled off the bus and then came the 'trainspotting' moment! There was shite all here! Well, that's not strictly true as there was a cafe, a visitor centre and a few shops. The cafe and centre were open, but the shops were all closed due to the 'non tourist' season.

'When's the next bus back?' Daryl asked.

'Too long!' Mike replied.

We all looked at each other and burst out laughing.

My second 'trainspotting' moment was at Savage River in Denali National Park. Again, getting off the bus, we looked around at our surroundings. Savage River didn't look at all 'savage' and it was bitterly cold. We were in the Tundra which, in itself, is amazing, however with the cold and rain, we didn't really appreciate it as much as we should have. The Tundra is an exceptional ecosystem which, only the hardiest of plants and wildlife thrive in the harsh conditions. I liked the fact that this was as far as road traffic could venture, leaving the wild to remain wild and unspoilt.

It was a place I would have loved to explore on foot with all our walking kit on, but with Mike's bad knee, we were only able to wander around close to the bus. Soon, we were back on the warm bus and heading back to the campsite.

Back at the tent and although it was only late afternoon, Mike set about lighting a fire in the fire pit to warm us both up. This is Mike's favourite task when camping, his job, man's work and all that! I'm pretty good at lighting a fire as well but I'm happy to humour Mike and let him get on with it.

"Ouch!" Man makes fire, Man chops wood, Man chops finger! Turning around to see Mike nursing his bleeding finger and once I'd checked that the finger wasn't hanging off, my next thought was, *guess who's getting out of doing dishes for a while??*

It was the day we were leaving Denali and still hadn't seen the mountain from the park but at least we got to see it from 30,000 feet up whilst flying. Although it was still chilly, at least the rain had stopped so packing up the tent wasn't a chore.

The park warden wandered by and asked where we were from. As soon as he heard that we were Scottish, he got onto the subject of whisky. Being three quarters Irish descent and a quarter German, Fritz (that's his German part!) told us about his visit to Ireland. While Fritz toured around Ireland, he liked to check out the Irish pubs.

"Wherever you go in the world, there are Irish pubs, so why not visit the real thing?" he explained. The first pub Fritz walked into was a small, quaint establishment in a country village.

Fritz enjoyed a particular tipple, *"Do you know how to make an Irish Car Bomb?"* he asked the bartender.

Fritz went on to tell us about the sudden hush in the pub and the bartender looking somewhat shocked as he didn't know of the drink, but he knew what a car bomb was. This was Ireland, for crying out loud!

Luckily the landlord knew of the drink; half a pint of Guinness, a shot glass of half Baileys and half Jamieson whisky. After making Fritz his Irish car bomb, he suggested that he didn't ask for that particular drink ever again in Ireland!

"And did you?" I asked Fritz.

"No, I kinda guessed that if I wanted to get outta Ireland in one piece, I should just stick to straight whisky!"

So, although the weather in Denali wasn't the best and we could have visited warmer parts of Alaska, that's not us. The weather was shite but Denali was spectacular; without doubt, a wild and beautiful place.

After Denali, we headed north on the Parks Highway towards Fairbanks. On either side of us, endless forests as far as the eye could see. Seeing the signpost for the small town of Nenana, I wondered why the name was familiar. Then it came to me; Mike's Alaska programme, *Life Below Zero.*

It's a wonder Mike's not wanting to drop in and see someone for a coffee! I thought to myself, smiling.

Seriously though; he watches the programme so much, it's not beyond possibility that Mike would know a couple of residents! We did stop in Nenana very briefly for an early lunch, aka warm up! The quaint little cafe was warm and welcoming; a lady welcomed us and poured us hot coffee straight away.

The couple at the next table saw me trying to warm my hands with the mug of coffee, *"It sure is cold out there,"* the lady said.

Nodding, I asked, *"Is it always this cold in June?"*

"It's usually warmer than this, but it's been strange weather of late," she replied.

For me, that was a glimmer of hope. Potentially, the weather should improve as the summer settled in. Feeling better after the positive news that the cold spell was unusual and not the norm, that and the homemade French toast with maple syrup, we left Nenana onwards to Fairbanks.

Soon we reached the city limits of Fairbanks, another name from the Alaska programme and also the last city for quite a while. I was feeling quite excited about the prospect of leaving civilization behind. Fairbanks was really a place to stop for fuel and provisions, and not for sightseeing. I'm sure that there's much to see and do in Fairbanks, however, it's a city and the trip's not about built up areas.

Another reason for stopping off in Fairbanks was to collect our Hoodoo beer glasses from the brewery. We were heading to Chickenstock, a famous music festival held in Chicken each year. The Hoodoo brewery was supplying the beer at the festival and, included in our tickets, we received a beer glass each. Our whistle-stop tour of Fairbanks done, we were back on the road, this time to Chena Hot Springs and further into Interior Alaska.

Discovered by gold prospectors in 1905, Chena Hot Springs has been a popular destination for people wanting to enjoy the health benefits of the waters since then. I could imagine during the long, dark winter months with freezing temperatures, the joy of soaking in the natural hot springs.

Would it make staying in Alaska during the winter enticing? No, not for me!

After riding along a scenic road for about an hour, we arrived at Chena Hot Springs. The road pretty much ends there and the scenery is quite spectacular with tree covered mountains, however the springs weren't what we had imagined.

Mike had an image in his head of a holiday spa resort and I pictured it to be a bit like Liard Hot Springs, basic, beautiful and natural. We both couldn't be more wrong as, although the surrounding countryside is beautiful, the resort was 'random' and well, disappointing. It's as if someone came along and threw a collection of buildings, greenhouses, cabins etc into the air and left them where they landed! And, why not throw in a dirt runway for aircraft right by the RV site with a large DC6 aircraft parked by the runway? Checking the aircraft out, Mike decided that it was the one featured in the *Life Below Zero* programme.

There were a couple of areas designated for tents, one of which was by the runway. I had visions of us in our tent as the plane took off, along with us! We opted for the other tent space by a little burn. It sounds idyllic but really wasn't; I would rather have been in the wilderness completely or in a proper campsite.

Just on the off chance that the price would be affordable, I asked the receptionist how much it would be to stay in either a cabin or the hotel itself. Too much was the answer. The good news was that we were allowed to use the facilities in the hotel and there was a restaurant and bar. Since we were saving on accommodation, we decided to splash out on eating in the restaurant and sitting in the bar.

The hotel itself was quite Germanic, wooden and in a Bavarian style of which we were used to from our years of living in Germany.

We'd arrived quite late so it would be the next day that we could enjoy the springs and do a spot of horse riding, western style.

The next morning wasn't any warmer but, at least we were dressed for the weather and we're outdoor people; the weather is what it is.

Stepping out of the tent, I noticed a movement in the bushes opposite.

"Mike," I whispered, loud enough for him to hear me without scaring whatever was lurking in the bushes.

Was it a bear, maybe? I was thinking.

Keeping an eye on the bushes which were swaying slightly, I noticed Mike join me, looking over to where I was pointing.

The bushes moved even more and out wandered a female moose all the while, grazing. And, what should trustingly follow her out, a calf!

"Oh, Mike, that's amazing!" I whispered, excitedly.

Mike's silence, but smiling, confirmed that he was as excited as me; he just shows it differently. We make a good team, yin and yang, Hazel says. I can be overly excited, and Mike, in his silent way, calms me down, or so he thinks!

The moose and her calf, not feeling threatened by us or just used to people camping here, continued calmly on their way, baby staying close by mum.

Still on a high after seeing the moose, (meese for plural?) I wandered over to the washrooms in the hotel. There was no designated dish washing area, so I took our breakfast plates and cups hidden in a rucksack to wash them in the sink in the toilet as well. Again, as before, campsites tend to cater for RVs which have their own built in sinks. I don't know what they expect campers to do, but to improvise.

The health benefits that the waters offer are renowned as long as you don't mind smelling like rotten eggs! And the taste of the water is particularly rank, healthy but rank!

Horse trekking first, or soaking in the hot springs and then on the horses? That was actually an easy one to decide as we both hadn't been riding for years; soaking in the waters afterwards might ease any aches and pains! The outdoor centre and stables were directly opposite the hotel, by the makeshift runway. While we waited for our guide and horses, we got chatting to Nate who worked there. I'm not sure if Nate's hair was meant to have the 'just got out of bed' look, or he really had just got out of bed and didn't feel the need to brush his hair! Nate's demeanour favoured the latter!

After Nate told us that he grew up in Philadelphia, I asked him what brought him this far north to Chena.

"It was the end of the road and my car broke down. I've been here for two years," he replied quite seriously, *"it's kinda hard to get a broken car outta here,"* he continued.

I did ask!

"Where you guys heading after Chena?" Nate asked

"Have you heard of Chickenstock Music Festival?" I asked, *"We're going there next"*

"No way! So am I!" Nate answered, smiling. *"Hey, I might see you there,"* he continued

Would we see Nate again at Chickenstock?

We met Elisa, our guide, a southerner from Texas. She was relatively new to Chena and arrived in February from kinder temperatures in Texas, to snow in Alaska. I'm amazed that she didn't turn around and go back home!

Elisa handed Mike his horse, Sarah. *"I'm sorry Mike, but Sarah has a gas problem!"*

"Just like her rider then!" I laughed. Unfortunately, I was riding on Coby who always followed Sarah, the gassy horse. That teaches me for trying to be funny!

It took awhile for me to get used to my horse his quirky ways. Mike and Elisa were getting further ahead and I was lagging behind. I knew there was some kind of trick to urge Coby to go faster, but I had to find it fast before I was left behind completely.

"Come on Coby," I whispered in his ear, *"Giddy up"*

Almost giving up hope, I touched him on a certain part of his side and, immediately we were cantering. *Found it!*

It didn't take us long to catch up with Mike and Elisa who were deep in conversation. *Hey, guys! I'm back, if you hadn't realised!!!* I felt like saying.

The trail we were on was a narrow one, so although I was right behind the others, I couldn't hear what they were chatting about. However, I was more than happy riding along on Coby, all the while looking out for any movements in the bushes.

At the end of the hack, back at the activity centre, I was sure that Coby and I had bonded. Dismounting, I noticed a conveniently placed sign, *'If you enjoyed the ride, kiss your horse and tip your guide'*

Nah! That's a step too far, I thought. Instead, I thanked Coby by rubbing his neck gently.

After horse riding, Mike and I went our separate ways; me for a hike and Mike off to Beaver Pond with his telescopic rod to try a spot of fishing. As in Scotland, fishing is permitted in Alaska, as long as you buy a fishing pass which Mike had done before leaving home.

"I'm not happy with you walking by yourself out here," Mike said, *"This is bear country."*

"I'm not the one fishing!" I replied, *"I know which one of us, I would go after if I was a bear!"* I continued.

Nevertheless, Mike insisted that I took the bear spray, which I have to admit, I was glad of. I actually wouldn't have gone walking without the spray, but I would have bought another one so that we had one each.

Mike headed out on his bike to Beaver Pond and I went off hiking deciding that I would walk to Beaver Pond and check that Mike was OK. This was indeed bear country.

Walking along a trail, there was nothing stirring in the bushes but my senses were heightened, just in case. The sun, for the first time in days, had 'burnt' through the clouds and the day was warming up nicely, and feeling like summer.

Seeing Mike up ahead standing at the pond casting his fishing line, I sneaked up to him just to check that his senses were tuned to his surroundings. They were and he knew instinctively that it was me and not a grizzly wanting to steal his fish.

"Where's your fish?" I asked.

Looking disappointed, he replied, *"I don't think there's anything worth catching in this pond."*

Shading my eyes with my hands, I scanned the still

waters. The only movement, that of insects skating across the surface of the pond and dragonflies hovering above.

Empty handed, Mike packed up his fishing gear and I headed back along the trail to the tent.

A short while later, the sound of dogs howling in the not too far distance got me wondering, *what's riled them?*

Ten minutes later, I got my answer. Up ahead careering towards me was a team of dogs pulling a sled with wheels on it and a bunch of tourists. Standing to the side, I watched them race past me, the dogs with their eyes wide with excitement. The tourists, all with their mobile phones, videoing the experience.

What's happened to people that they feel that they have to photograph or video everything? Why not just enjoy the experience and capture the memory through our eyes?

Meeting back at the tent and gathering our swimming things together, we headed over to the Hot Springs. Again, I was struck by how different Chena Hot Springs was compared to Liard. Here, although the waters were completely natural, the way it's set up, is almost artificial. Sinking into the water with the heat relaxing all my muscles, I didn't care; this was bliss!

As we wandered around the pool, there were hot spots where the water feels almost boiling and only bearable for seconds at a time.

This was the warmest I'd been since Anchorage and I was enjoying every minute of it. Body relaxed, fingers going all wrinkled with the water, we reluctantly waded out of the water and dried ourselves. Smelling of rotten eggs and feeling amazing, this was the end of a perfect day.

The next morning, early, we packed up to leave Chena, via Fairbanks for Tok, a 249 mile ride. The stop in Fairbanks would be another quick stop to buy plenty of food for the weekend in Chicken.

There was a definite chill in the air, and checking the thermometer, it was three degrees celcius.

Riding from Chena, I kept glancing at the temperature gauge, hoping that it would warm up. Today would depend on whether the sun would appear from behind the cloudy, grey skies. And sure enough, when the sun was out, the temperature crept up slightly, but dipped whenever the sun disappeared behind the clouds.

Up ahead, we both saw a moose in front of us, blocking the way. We slowed to a stop, giving the moose plenty of space. These huge animals could trample us quite easily, and the last thing we wanted was to intrude in its space and then for it to charge at us.

Sitting astride our bikes, the engines purring just in case we needed to make a quick getaway, we watched the beautiful creature. She looked at us quite calmly and then started ambling towards us which, was when we readied ourselves even more to try and go around her. She stopped and looked like she was thinking about her next move; then turned to the side and disappeared gracefully into the trees.

To the moose, she's not crossing a road, she's making her way through the forest which man has decided to build a road through!

Although the temperature had risen by a couple of degrees, by the time we reached Fairbanks, my hands were numb with the cold.

The temperature was just above freezing and I've inherited my dad's condition, Raynaud's. Cold weather or stress can cause arteries to narrow leaving extremities to go numb and then painful. I wasn't stressed, far from it, so it had to be the weather. Even my thick motorbike gloves weren't helping; I was worried.

Getting off my bike in a supermarket car park, Mike knew straight away that something was wrong. *"Right, we need to get you some thicker gloves!"*

In the supermarket, we went our separate ways; Mike to get the food shopping while I scoured the aisles for gloves.

Asking a sales assistant where the gloves would be, she

said, *"No, we don't have any left as its summer now."*
Has she been outside recently, or is she a tough Alaskan? Just as I thought I had no chance of finding anything, I spotted a pair of snowboard gloves in the sales section. Even though they looked like lobster claws, they were perfect! I found Mike, who, by this time, had a trolley full of food to be packed on the bikes.

Showing Mike the gloves, he asked how much they were. To be honest, I hadn't even looked at the price, I just knew that I needed these gloves to be able to continue on the trip with warm hands.

Turning the gloves over, I couldn't see any price tag. We took them to the checkout along with the food, hoping that the sales assistant would know. When she went to scan the gloves and finding no price, she called her supervisor.

"I'm sorry but we can't sell you these gloves. There's no price on them."

"But they were in the sales section, so they must be for sale," I suggested.

The supervisor then contacted the shop manager for advice. Mike and I, by this time, were both bemused and frustrated.

Luckily the shop manager had common sense and told us a price for the gloves; ten cents! Deal!

With warmer hands and our panniers filled to the brim with provisions, we left Fairbanks and continued our journey to Tok for the night. There was one place en-route, however, that we just had to do; North Pole! Not *The* North Pole, but North Pole, Alaska, 17 miles outside Fairbanks.

When the town was called North Pole, little did the townsfolk know that this would put the community 'on the map'. Today North Pole is a popular tourist attraction, especially during the summer months, strangely enough!

And in North Pole of course, there has to be a Santa Claus House which I wanted to visit.

Walking into Santa Claus House was walking into Christmas itself. Turning around to smile at Mike, I saw that his face was tripping him. He is a typical *bah humbug* and our whole family know it and we all find it amusing.

The Christmas shopping is left to me apart from my present that is, and this is usually bought online from the comfort of Mike's chair, probably whilst watching a programme about Alaska!

I have to admit, though, that after a short while in the Santa Claus House, the constant Christmas music was starting to get on my nerves. It wasn't Christmas, it was summer! We were really only there to buy two letters from Santa in North Pole for our granddaughters. Letters bought, coffee drunk and obligatory photo at North Pole signpost; we were back on our bikes heading to Tok.

From North Pole, this had to be the most boring part of the trip so far. The road, straight and not much in the way of countryside to look at. One highlight which broke up the boredom of the ride was seeing the military jets flying above us as we rode past Eilsen Airbase. Dogfighting in the skies above our heads, I was humming, *Jet planes flying high above me;* it was quite exhilarating.

The closer we rode to Tok, the warmer the weather was becoming and it felt more like summer by the time we arrived in Tok itself.

Although a small town, there was a vibrant feel to it. The aroma of fresh baking hit us as we walked into the campsite office.

The receptionist greeted us smiling, *"Come in, come in. Welcome to Tok. Here, have a cookie; they're just out of the oven!"*

What a lovely welcome, I thought.

The still warm biscuit was delicious, chewy and exactly what I needed after a few hours on the bike!

We were seeing more and more riders on the road, and here in Tok, we were camped right by six other bikers who were all heading the opposite way, south.

Tok was merely a stopover en-route to Chicken however, I

don't think there was that much to see or do in the town; it seemed to thrive as a place to stop for a break.

We didn't wake up late the following morning, but our neighbours had already left; we were the only bikers left. I must've slept soundly as I hadn't even heard their engines as they left.

Turning left after Tok, we continued our journey on the Taylor Highway heading towards Chicken. Finally leaving civilisation behind, this was more like it; panoramic views of forests stretching out as far as the eye could see. Out of the green vegetation, black spruce ravaged by wildfires stood where they had once flourished. It seems sad when wildfires happen, but I read that it's sometimes nature's way of enriching the earth for the new vegetation to grow. The circle of life.

No matter how much I looked as we rode along, I saw no signs of wildlife. I've realised that this country is so massive, that the animals don't have to venture near roads and therefore, people. Whenever we've seen bears on our last jaunts, it's been during the autumn when they're busy eating berries, fattening up for the impending winter; and also in the spring time after the snows have melted and the bears are hungry. I'm staying positive that we will see some bears this time around.

The road to Chicken, as well as being more scenic and remote, was also in fairly good condition. The harsh winter had left its mark, however, with frost heaves and sections of the highway, so badly damaged, that gravel had been used to keep the road open. Small orange flags warned us of the gravel break we would be riding through. I've got history with deep gravel and try to avoid it as much as possible; I don't like it at all!

Each gravel patch we rode through, I tried not to tense up and said to myself, *you can do it Lynn*. And, you know what? I did it, and quite easily too. A real confidence booster, especially as a lot of the roads would be dirt.

TERMIGAN, TARMIGAN.... CHICKEN!

Chicken is a small settlement/community of around 120 people during the summer, but reduces to three during the long winter months. The road to Chicken, during the winter, is actually closed from October. The only sure way to reach the town during these months is by plane onto the small runway.

I thought that Mike was joking when he told me how Chicken got its name, but he wasn't! The story goes, that the first settlers/prospectors to Chicken wanted to name the town 'Ptarmigan' after the local bird but couldn't decide on the correct spelling.

One of the settlers said, *"It's just like a big chicken! Let's call the town, Chicken!"*
And, that's how the town got its name. Was alcohol involved in the decision making, I wonder?

Gold mining, still to this day, takes place in the surrounding hills, keeping Chicken, the town, alive. Something else that keeps the community 'on the map', when Chickenstock Music Festival comes to town, each summer, for a weekend.

The population increases massively with festival goers, and the logistics of accommodating the onslaught of folk, must be a task in itself!

Mike had planned ahead and bought tickets for the festival and managed to reserve one of the last, secluded tent spaces away from the crowds.

Turning right off the Highway, we rode down into Chicken, and sure enough, there was a chicken! Not a real chicken, but a large metal one standing on top of a hillock, dominating the town. A wild west gun-toting town called Chicken, why wouldn't they have a chicken as the town symbol? The grassy knoll where the structure was, later would be covered with tents, haphazardly erected, with hardly any grass left showing.

Seeing a steady stream of people going in and out of a wooden building, we guessed that this must be the registration point for festival goers. Parking our bikes outside, it was so busy with folk that it was easy to forget that we really were in the outback here in Chicken. No point checking the one mobile phone we brought for the trip; there's no phone coverage here. What about emergencies?

There's a satellite phone for that! If our granddaughter was born this weekend, we wouldn't know about it until we reached Dawson City.

Inside the building, which served as a cafe and gift shop, Mike went to register us while I browsed around the shop. I saw, then, that it was a well executed set up to cope with the arrivals all flocking to Chicken.

Chickenstock, music on *top of the world,* is the first festival I've attended; and it's fair to say that I wasn't sure if I was going to enjoy it, or not. Time would tell.

Having registered, we hopped on our bikes and made our way to our designated tent site. Riding up a dirt track through the trees, we turned right which took us down over rocky ground to a clearing on the right. When I saw our site, I felt relief wash over me; it was perfect! Secluded, clean and surrounded by trees, I couldn't have wished for better. And the best bit; it was a short two minute walk to where the festival was taking place.

Jumping for joy, once I'd parked my bike that is; I glanced at the ground and noticed moose pooh. This day was getting even better we would no doubt see some moose as well.

To one side of us, through the trees, was another tent space which was empty at the moment. Further down the hillside, a tepee style tent was already erected and the occupants were 'at home'. How did we know they were in their tent? The unmistakable, pungent smell of cannabis, heavy in the air, wafting from the tent was a pretty good clue!

After pitching the tent, we ventured to watch the goings on and to relax with a drink; I was enjoying that 'weekend' feeling. It wasn't long before we got chatting to Ted, a local guy and volunteer working for the festival.

Mike asked Ted about fishing in the local area and just had to also ask about the firearm in Ted's holster! Once Ted found out that we were from the UK, he introduced us to Simon; another Brit. Simon was also ex-military and had moved to Alaska a number of years ago. Before we knew it, he was away in his ATV, delivering firewood to our campsite. As ever, we were blown away by people's generosity.

Sitting on the wooden decked veranda with our drinks, it was just nice to watch the goings-on. How often, in life, do we simply sit and observe? Just recently, after our trip, I was in a huge shopping centre in England.

Waiting for Mike, I stood and watched the hustle and bustle of the shoppers. It's times like these when you realise where or what you would rather be doing. In that shopping centre with, what seemed like hundreds of people and the intense, almost unbearable noise, I knew that this wasn't where I wanted to be!

The shoppers rushing past me looked unhappy, and the children, in-tow, certainly would rather have been spending their day somewhere else. I thought of Chicken, Alaska that day in the shopping centre; not of the place, but of the feeling of peace I felt there. I know that I don't have to go back to Chicken to feel that sense of contentment; spending time with my family or walking in the woods with my dog is, for me, contentment, my happy place.

Back on the veranda in Chicken, I was struck by the mix of people milling around the small community. When I think of festival goers, I imagine groups of young people or, at least like minded folk gathering together. At Scone Palace, they host a festival called Rewind, 80's music. I don't like stereotyping people, but, during Rewind, we can tell the festival goers from the tourists visiting a stately home! Think 80's clothes and you'll know what I mean!

But, here at Chickenstock, there's folk of all ages, from children to the elderly. The only one mutual sameness they all have in common, and that is denim or Carhartt clothing; functional, practical and hard wearing.

Scanning the crowd, something caught my eye.

No way! Is that someone gold panning?

Sitting up, I focused on the people stooped over a wooden trough.

"Mike. Look over there!" I said, excitedly, pointing over to the people.

"They're panning for gold. Let's go and watch"

With hands in the dirty, clay water, a lady was busy searching for the precious metal we still, to this day, have a fascination for; gold.

We stood stock still, watching her swirl the water and separate the stones and the light sandy soil until, finally, she was left with the dark silt. With filthy fingers, she moved the dirt about until, there, gleaming out of the dark earth, were a few tiny flakes of gold. While her partner continued to swirl and sift in silence; the lady was happy to explain the process of panning for gold.

"You see, gold is 19 times heavier than water, so the gold will sink to the bottom. So, first you gotta try and separate the light, sandy soil from the water."

As I watched her hands swirl in the grey water, I was amazed that she didn't seem to feel the cold.

Without looking up from the task in hand, she continued, *"so, looky there. Here's where the gold will be hiding, in this dark silt."*

Sure enough, the sandy soil and stones had been removed, and there glinting out of the silt, tiny flakes of gold!

"Ya see it?" she pointed to the gold.

I could hardly believe what I was seeing; gold that's stayed hidden for hundreds of thousands of years. I now had an insight as to how the prospectors must've felt when they first struck gold, and how addictive it was.

Looking at the rest of the cloudy water, I wondered how much more gold was just waiting to be discovered in the trough. The very thought of keeping my hands in cold water for any length of time, even for gold, wasn't worth it, to me anyway.

Thanking her for sharing her knowledge and obvious passion for the search of gold; we wandered up the hill to the local inn. Sitting outside, beer in hand, was a familiar face; Nate from Chena!

"Hey, guys. You made it to Chickenstock!" Nate greeted us.

Nate's hair was even more dishevelled than two days ago in Chena. This was taking bed hair to the extreme.

"Hi Nate," I replied, trying not to stare at his hair which, was standing vertical from his head!

We chatted for a few minutes, but it was obvious that Nate was a popular guy so we said our goodbyes and left him with his friends, all female, I hasten to add!

Although the festival itself didn't kick off until the next day, there was already a carnival atmosphere to this Alaskan outpost. My previous doubts about the festival were disappearing; taking a deep breath, looking around me, I took a moment to capture this feeling.

This is amazing! We're here, in Alaska, at a festival on top of the world!

On our first trip to the USA, we got chatting to an American lady, "*You Europeans have got so much history; we don't have that here in the States.*"

Slightly bemused, but not wanting to question her statement, I thought about what she had said. I think I understood what she was meaning however, it was a nonsensical thing to say. Everywhere has history; whether it's yesterday, last month or a 100 years ago; it's happened so therefore; it's history.

The town of Chicken breathes history; days of the Gold Rush, hardship, survival and community.

Dominating the skyline of Chicken is the Pedro Gold Dredge, an abandoned, wooden and steel structure which, in its heyday, mined over 55,000 ounces of gold. This is no *Eiffel Tower,* dapper through the day and dressed to the nines at night; the Dredge is more of a mishmash monster which tells a story of the gold rush era and striking it rich or not, as was often the case. For me, dredging conjures up negative images of the destruction of natural habitats and the ecosystem however, I'm sure there's times and places where dredging may be beneficial. Dredge #4, has found its permanent resting place in Chicken and now serves as a museum, open to the public and bringing in much needed cash to this small outpost on the Taylor Highway.

Another peek into the past is Historic Chicken, the original village which, although on private land, is on the National Register of Historic Places and open to the public, albeit at a small charge. Wherever we go on our travels, if we find a particular place interesting, Mike and I like to take a tour, usually guided by someone local to that area.

Setting off with our guide from The Goldpanner Gift Shop, we were the only people booked in for the tour of old Chicken. Following the guide across the Taylor Highway, I couldn't help checking both ways for traffic; I put it down to habit. Traffic on the Taylor Highway?

Sure, there may be the occasional vehicle, moose or bear, but you could probably lie down in the middle of the road for a while before anything came along! Now, I'm not suggesting that lying across a road, is a good idea, so, folks, don't try this at home or in Alaska; actually, not a good idea at all, anywhere!

Nestled behind shrubbery and bushes, a collection of rickety cabins that made up Chicken came into view. A ghost town since 1967 and, for the most part, undisturbed, nature has reclaimed old Chicken.

"*We'd best look out for moose,*" our guide whispered, breaking the silence.

Sure enough there, in the dirt track, moose tracks.

"*These ponds here are favourite drinking spots for the moose,*" she continued, pointing to small pools of still water.
And a breeding ground for mosquitoes! I thought, noticing the blood sucking gnats hovering over the stagnant water.

We wandered from cabin to cabin, all the while, hearing tales of when this was a thriving community. Some of the cabins were too dangerous and unstable to enter, however, one that we were able to go into was *Tisha's School House.*

This had to be, for me, the most memorable cabin we visited. Here, we heard about Anne Hobbs, a young teacher, who came to Chicken to educate the children. Only 19 years old and new to the Alaskan wilderness, Anne not only faced the harsh winter, but also the attitudes and prejudices of the townsfolk against the native children being taught by Anne in the schoolhouse. Anne remained true to her belief that all children were entitled to an education, no matter where they came from. Her nickname, Tisha, came about when one of her native pupils, Chuck, couldn't pronounce *Teacher* properly and it sounded like *Tisha.*

If I could go back in time, Anne is someone I would like to meet. I'm reading her biography at the moment, which is fascinating and I can picture how the empty schoolhouse we visited, must have been when Anne lived and taught there. The book is also a love story, but I'll leave it at that and not spoil it for anyone who fancies reading *Tisha.*

Leaving the Gold Rush days behind, we fast-forward to present day, 2018 and Chickenstock Music Festival!

Sitting on our camping chairs, we waited with bated breath for the launch of the festival. The DJ, microphone in hand and dressed as a chicken, announced Chickenstock 2018, officially open.

Two old, rusty mining trucks, back to back, supported a rickety looking wooden platform; this was the stage, Alaskan style. The performers, some bands and other solo artists, took turns to play to the audience. Music filled the air in Chicken that weekend, a mixture of country rock, Bluegrass and folk.

Looking around, I was surprised at how many families were here for the festival. While the parents danced and enjoyed the music, their children were playing happily on the steep, dusty hill behind the stage. By the end of the day, they were filthy, but happy. No televisions or internet; just playing in the sandy earth with sticks.

At one point through the day, a small four year old boy went missing; a parent's worst nightmare. Whereas, in other places, thoughts of the child being taken by some low life might cross people's minds, in Chicken, the fear was of the wee lad being trampled by moose, attacked by a bear or other dangers of wilderness Alaska. The word spread quickly and soon, the festival goers and organisers had forgotten the music, and were searching for the boy; humanity at its best. The lad had just wandered off and was soon found playing in the bush; the panic stricken parents were visibly relieved and the music resumed.

While the younger children played in the dirt with

sticks, the older teenagers danced and twirled with hula hoops in time to the music. I admit to being slightly jealous; I had never been able to use a hula hoop. And yet, here, in Chicken, I was determined to master this skill. Waiting until one of the hula hoops was left on the ground; I picked it up and stepped inside the ring. Mike looked at me, shaking his head, but smiling.

He didn't think I'd do it. *I'll show him! I'm going to hula hoop!* I told myself.

I gyrated, determined to keep the hoop going, and although, clumsy and ungainly, I did it!

When we came back, I bought a hula hoop and haven't looked back. The neighbours in the village are used to seeing me twirling around the garden with my hoop and headphones on. Or, at work, I'll quite often hula hoop during quiet spells; (definitely quiet times Heather, aka, my Manager)!

During the festival, we kept hearing folk talk about the main act, Cousin Curtis. We had never heard of him, but he seemed to be a popular singer. Cousin Curtis was a local guy who used to teach in Tok, but found success in the music industry.

As soon as Cousin Curtis took to the stage, I liked him, and that was before he started singing. He had an infectious smile and seemed a genuinely nice guy. I just hoped that I was going to like his music. Playing the guitar, Cousin Curtis's first song had the audience, including me, up dancing and singing along. Now, I knew why Cousin Curtis was the main act and so popular; a local guy, great singer and, the best quality about him; he hadn't forgotten his roots.

During a break in the music, there was an announcement from the DJ, *"I hate to tell you this folks, but we've run out of IPA,"* (beer!)

Before the crowd could protest, he continued, *"it's in hand, don't worry. We've sent a plane down to Fairbanks to the brewery to get more!"*

The initial worried faces in the crowd turned to smiles

when they knew that more beer was on the way.

Only in Alaska, I thought.

True to his word, an hour or so later, the DJ interrupted the music again. *"Look up there folks!"* he announced pointing up to a small plane coming in to land, *"there's the beer plane!"* An enormous cheer came from the crowd and someone shouted, *"the IPA has landed!"* That brought even more cheering and clapping; beer problem resolved, the music started up again.

From being nervous about going to the festival, to not wanting it to end; I'd had an amazing time. But, it wasn't over yet; I still had the Chicken Run to complete. This was a five kilometre run or walk around Chicken, starting with a steep hill and then into the bush.

I've taken part in a lot of fun runs, but never one where we were told to be careful of bear and moose! Mike stayed behind waiting for me to finish, I felt bad about that; he would have loved to take part but he couldn't because of his knee.

Another highlight of Chickenstock was the Peep Drop. We had no idea what a Peep was, let alone a Peep Drop! Mike and I set about finding out and could hardly believe what we were told, *"They drop marshmallow chickens out of a plane over our heads."*

Dancing to Cousin Curtis, the DJ shouted over the music that the plane was heading our way. We all looked up and the plane flew just 50 feet above our heads; this was a practice run.

We watched as the plane turned and made its way back to us. The crowd cheered the plane on, waving their arms in the air. Again, with the plane only 50 feet above us, this time, marshmallow chicken peeps, rained down over our heads! Carried along by the excitement of the crowd, Mike and I tried to catch the chickens, but failed miserably. What an amazing and strange end to Chickenstock.

When Mike posted on Facebook about the Peep Drop, a friend of mine asked, *"Chicken!? Like, their corpses???"*

"No, Carol; no chickens were harmed in the Peep Drop!"

Chickenstock 2018 was over and it was time for us to head off to our next destination, Eagle, another place from the Alaskan programme, *Life Below Zero.*

The road sign on leaving Chicken, reads 'Pavement Ends'; no more tarmac for quite a while. The road from here, was going to be more of a challenge; bring it on!

Keeping warm in
Chicken

Whenever we told people we met along the way that we were riding down to Eagle, we were told horror stories about the road to Eagle.

"Man, that's a scary road" or *"It took us hours to get to Eagle"* or *"The road is so narrow."*

With these warnings in our heads, we turned left off the main route and headed towards Eagle. The 65 mile dirt road to Eagle was probably my favourite ride this trip around.

Yes, in places it was a bit cheeky, but no way did either of us think it was scary. The road, at times, hugged the mountain side and looking way down, the views were spectacular. We couldn't really see much as the road did mean that sightseeing was a no no.

By the time we reached Eagle, I was covered in the dust kicked up from riding behind Mike; dusty but happy! The road ended at Eagle so, the next day, we would be riding back up the same road; I was already looking forward to that.

Situated on the banks of the Yukon and overlooked by a cliff called Eagle Bluff, the small town of Eagle is home to approximately 84 people. A quaint little hamlet, straight away, I liked the atmosphere in the town.

We parked by a modern looking building, Riverside Hotel, which turned out to also be the general store, hardware store and restaurant. The previous hotel was swept away in the 2009 flood during a particularly bad ice break up.

Having stocked up on provisions for the night, we rode to the State run campsite. Riding through the wooded site, it was easy to find our spot for the night. Although basic, surrounded by trees and secluded, our home for the night was idyllic.

On the way up to the campsite, we had spotted the National Park Service office; a *must go to* place for information in the local area. Once the tent was up, Mike and I headed back to the Park office where we met June, the Ranger on duty that day.

I asked June if she could recommend a small hike in the area near the campsite.

"Sure, there's a pretty nice walk to Beaver Pond," she suggested.

"Are there beavers in Beaver Pond?" Mike asked.

"There were," June replied, *"up until four years ago,"* she continued.

Seeing our confused expressions, June explained further, *"Beaver Pond had beavers there until Fred Squirrels trapped them."*

"What?" I said, all of a sudden, feeling sad.

"He was told to leave the beavers be. We all hunt, it's Alaska for crying out loud, but those beavers were popular to folk visiting here. There's no point having a pond called Beaver Pond with no darn beavers in it!"

June was clearly not happy with Fred Squirrels and it seems that the rest of the town felt the same, *"We've never forgiven Fred for what he did to the beavers."*

The hike sounded nice, so we decided that we would still go to Beaver Pond anyway. June also told us about tours of historic Eagle, so we booked in for that for the following morning.

Following June's directions, we started down a dirt track through the trees. Mindful of this being bear country, the bear spray was to hand, just in case.

It wasn't too long before we came upon the small wooden bridge June had told us about. What June hadn't warned us about was how bad the mosquitoes would be at this particular point of the walk. They were vicious, huge and liked Mike!

"Aw, shit! What was that?" I said, wildly looking around, getting ready to run at the gunshot like sound.

"Someone's shooting!" I said, in a loud whisper, imagining Fred Squirrels hiding in the bushes!

Mike, calm and collected, stopped. *"That's a beaver slapping its tail,"* he said smiling.

Not convinced, I still followed Mike to the edge of Beaver Pond where the sound had come from. No Fred Squirrels, but the mosquitoes were lying in wait. Glancing over the surface of the pond, we saw something gliding through the water.

"There!" Mike whispered, pointing.

Sure enough, there in Beaver Pond, was a beaver!

"They're back! The beavers are back!"

The beavers knew that we were there and, to warn the other beavers, slapped its paddle like tail loudly on the surface of the water. That's what I had heard; the 'gunshot' was the beaver slapping its tail when they heard us near their home.

Mike took out his camera and started filming. Forgetting the attacking mosquitoes, we hunkered down and watched the beaver patrolling his or her pond.

"We'll have to tell June and show her the footage," Mike suggested.

"Definitely, but we'll have to swear her to secrecy and not tell Fred Squirrels!" I answered.

Staying longer to watch the beaver was tempting, but the mosquitoes were proving too bothersome and no amount of arm waving was keeping them away; they were after our Scottish blood!

Back at the tent, I set about cooking tea while Mike rode his bike further down the track to the crate of free firewood. It wasn't long before I heard the sound of the bike returning. Looking up, there was Mike, a big grin on his face, and strapped to the back of his bike, a stack of firewood! We were happy campers who would be toasty warm this evening.

Although we were on holiday, we weren't drinking wine every evening however, tonight, in Eagle, we would enjoy a glass of wine by the fire in the forest. Eagle is a damp community; nothing to do with the weather! In the USA, there are dry, damp and wet communities. It's all about alcohol and some villages/towns trying to control the sale and consumption of it.

Modern day prohibition! We weren't aware of any dry communities on our travels, where the sale, possession and consumption of alcohol is banned. Someone had told us, in advance, that Eagle is a damp town; drinking is allowed but there's nowhere to buy it. No worries there; we had bought a bottle of wine in Tok, with Eagle in mind. Then, the wet towns are the normal communities where alcohol isn't restricted, apart from the usual regulations.

Being European, this just seems archaic to us, especially when some of these States allow cannabis and, of course, there's the firearms issue. You can shoot a gun and use cannabis, but alcohol? No, that's way too dangerous!

The following day, we woke early to pack up before heading down to the meeting point for the tour of historic Eagle, outside the Courthouse Museum.

On the tour with us, were three other visitors and the guide, an elderly local man. The guide walked slowly through the town, pointing out historic points of interest. I don't know whether he walked slowly because he was old, or there's no need to rush in Eagle.

The guide even spoke slowly, so I would like to think that it was the latter; why rush in this tiny hamlet?

The town has an alpine feel to it, lush green meadows with tiny, wild strawberries growing up through the grass. The reason for Eagle being there was down to the Gold Rush and the mighty Yukon River. In its heyday, Eagle was a busy trading post and was known as the *Paris of the North*. But once the Gold Rush was over, the population dropped from 1,500 to only around 200. Although its boomtown days were over, Eagle was home to a tight-knit community of hardy folk, which, it still is to this day.

The five restored buildings, including the Courthouse,

were open for the walking tour and crammed full of history. As interesting as the buildings were, nothing we saw could beat the guide's stories of days gone by in the town of Eagle.

Before we came to Eagle, I had wondered why Mike wanted to take a detour to visit the town, especially as it's one way in and back out the same route. But, after our stay there, I'm certainly glad that we did. Not only for the thrill of the ride into Eagle, but also for the town itself. If time allows, and you're passing by the turn off for Eagle, you won't be disappointed if you happen to find yourself taking that turn.

Riding out of Eagle, we took it in turns to ride in front; I didn't want the lion's share of the dust and dirt!

Back at Jack Wade Junction, we turned left towards Canada and Dawson City. We were about to ride the famous *Top of the World Highway*. Again, we were told varying accounts about the condition of the road, the views and generally, what to expect. Were the reviews correct? Yes, in some ways, but others, no, not really. I would imagine some of the advice would be weather dependant. Here's my experience of the *Top of the World Highway*.

The road leading towards the Border Control was beautifully paved; one of the smoothest I have ever ridden on. Crossing into Canada, the highway from there, for the most part, is gravel, but as it was dry that day, the road was absolutely fine for riding on. Another day when the weather isn't so kind, the ride would be a bit more challenging. I can also see why it's called *Top of the World Highway*, as that's how it feels; the views are spectacular and far reaching; the tree line, far below us.

To be honest, I preferred the Taylor Highway into Eagle and I've seen nicer views when riding through Scotland. That said, I still have fond memories of the *Top of the World Highway*, and that's a good thing.

Camping in Eagle

The road started dropping in altitude and, going around a slight bend, the Yukon River came into view. And there, on the far side, Dawson City; an actual real Wild West town.

Waiting for the George Black Ferry which would take us over to Dawson, we were soon joined by a few other bikes and some cars. No one was in a hurry; it was nice to just sit and ponder about stuff.

Before long, the ferry had reached our side, loaded us all up and headed back over the mighty Yukon. This well used and vital service is free to use, and seemed to be constantly back and forth the river.

Dawson City attracts hundreds of bikers in June around the Summer Solstice for the *Dust 2 Dawson (D2D)* Motorcycle Ride. D2D came about in 1992 as a tribute to a fallen friend, and since then has increased, each year, in popularity within the biking fraternity.

Whenever someone mentions D2D, they usually follow it up with *"it's Not a rally!"* This is just a fun couple of days, meeting old and new friends, all sharing the same passion for biking, with some motorcycle games, food and beer, of course!

Situated close to three of the best roads for riding, Dawson City is the obvious location for the Dust 2 Dawson meeting. Knowing how popular D2D is becoming, Mike had pre-booked the campsite, so that's where we headed first.

It seems that the campsites with more facilities are the least attractive and the tent spaces are bang next to each other. Although nice to have facilities such as showers and launderettes, I prefer camping in the woods, secluded from other people; I like my space (and, I'm just unsociable!). By the time we had reached Dawson City, we had not showered for three days and I think we still smelled OK! I was, however, looking forward to a hot shower and wash off the dust from the road.

Tent up in our allotted, tiny spot, a load of washing on and a welcome shower, we went off to discover Dawson City.

What a quirky little town! Dawson City truly is a town

stuck in the Wild West or Gold Rush days. The pavements are wooden boardwalks and the roads, dusty and unpaved. Had we walked into a film set? No, Dawson City is the real deal, with colourful wooden buildings such as Diamond Tooth Gertie and Bombay Peggy.

The only properties that aren't lived in, are known as the *Kissing buildings* due to the way they've snuggled up to each other as a result of the permafrost thawing from the heat within the buildings.

Completing the Wild West feeling was the wooden batwing doors leading into the Sourdough Saloon in the Downtown Hotel. It was easy to picture cowboys and miners walking through the double doors into a spit-and-sawdust saloon bar. There would be men playing poker, maybe some dancing girls and, of course, a lot of drinking. Fights and quarrels breaking out, especially after a few drinks or an unhappy loser at a poker game; tables would be upturned and the fight, often spilling out through the swing doors onto the dusty streets.

Walking through the swing doors was like walking into an old Western movie; the decor was typical of that period with an old tack piano sitting in the corner. We would be back that evening, not just to enjoy the ambience, but also for Mike to take the challenge of the Sourtoe Cocktail!

Visitors flock to the Sourdough Saloon to drink a shot of alcohol with a mummified human toe floating in it. The story goes that, in the 1920s, a man named Louie Linken, stepped into an icy overflow, plunging his foot into the glacial water. His big toe was frostbitten, and to prevent gangrene, he amputated it with an axe. Now, why he decided to preserve it in a jar of alcohol baffles me, but he did.

In 1973, Captain Dick Stevenson discovered the toe and so, the Sourtoe Cocktail Club was formed. People, still to this day, donate their toes to this club, which is then preserved in salt and brought out each evening for the initiation into the club.

Later that first evening in Dawson City, Mike bought his

shot, sat opposite Sourtoe Sue, paid his $5, the blackened toe was taken out of the salt and dropped into his drink.

Then came the famous words; *"You can drink it fast, you can drink it slow, but your lips must touch the toe!*

Mike downed the shot until his lips *kissed* the toe. A cheer rose from the crowd and he was presented with his certificate. The club is now onto its tenth toe and there's a fine if you swallow said toe! And, yes, that has actually happened!

Mike asked me, *"Are you going to take the challenge?"*

"I wouldn't kiss my own toe, let alone a dead one!" I replied

All the while, the old honky-tonk piano was being played by a little old man with no sheets of music to refer to. Watching his fingers dance effortlessly across the keys, it was evident that the gentleman was an old pro. Sure enough, chatting to someone in the bar, we found out that the pianist was an ex music teacher who now played each evening at the Sourdough Saloon, and lived out in the bush with just his dogs for company.

Exploring Dawson City, we realised that there was something missing; High Street Chains such as Starbucks, McDonalds etc. I'm not complaining at all; it was refreshing to see independent businesses thriving in this unique little town. But, how could this be? Why haven't the big names moved in? They're simply not allowed, that's why.

There's an old fashioned hardware store in Dawson, which sells individual nails and screws; not multiple packs. Our favourite store was the Trading Post; an Aladdin's Cave selling all sorts of merchandise. From wellies to antiques, the Trading Post seemed to stock practical and unusual things. Spotting some old, grainy black and white photographs in a pile on a shelf, I carefully sifted through them. Two of the photos caught my eye; one of a lady and the other, a man; there was something about their expressions, which intrigued me. A lady standing next to me in the Trading Post saw me looking at the photos.

"I wonder who they were?" she said.

I nodded, replying, *"Wouldn't it be nice to find out?"*

That's when I had the idea! Hazel, our daughter, has recently qualified as a primary school teacher and, after the holidays, will have her very own class of pupils. I told the lady about my idea, *"Wouldn't it be good to really look at the people in the photos; their expressions, and invent a life, a story for that person?"*

"My daughter could ask her pupils to write an essay about the person in the photo," I continued.

The lady agreed and so, I bought the photographs for Hazel's pupils. When I gave them to Hazel, telling her about my idea, she thought it was a great incentive for the children to get them using their imaginations.

Photos in hand and strolling along the boardwalks back to our tent, a Ford pick-up truck drove slowly by; no-one rushes in Dawson City! Nothing unusual there, apart from the dog standing on the roof, *surfing* as the truck moved down the street. Mike and I looked at each other, laughing. *Only in Dawson City,* I thought.

"How do you fancy going up to Tombstone?" Mike asked. This isn't Tombstone, Arizona; it's Tombstone Territorial Park in the Yukon; a beautiful and bewitching landscape. There's over 2000 kilometres of rugged mountains, sweeping valleys and an abundance of flora and fauna.

To reach Tombstone meant riding part way up the Dempster Highway, 700 kilometre dirt, gravel road which leads as far as the Arctic coast.

"Yes, definitely," I replied, even though inside I was feeling slightly nervous about riding on the Dempster. Yet again, I had listened to horror stories about the highway; that said, nothing was going to stop me from experiencing it for myself.

From Dawson City, we rode 40 kilometres up the North Klondike Highway, turning left onto the Dempster Highway. Slightly cautious at first, I soon realised that the Dempster was well within my capabilities as a rider. And yet, this is a road that should be treated with respect and not with a gung-ho attitude. Today was dry, a good day for riding the Dempster; a different story in wet weather when the road turns into a mud bath. We were only riding 71 kilometres of the Dempster, but riding all the way to the Arctic coast needs to be planned; where to fuel up, weather conditions, plenty of food and water, spare tyres and all-weather clothing.Taking the lead, I could feel the fine gravel moving under the tyres; this was fun!

An hour later, we reached Tombstone Interpretive Centre, an impressive building full of information about the park and the wildlife that roams the land.

After the Centre, we rode further up the Dempster to a viewpoint, recommended to us by the Park Ranger. Pulling over, this was the perfect spot for our picnic. The views looking down the valley were spectacular; an ancient land, untouched, pristine and vast. It was easy to imagine herds of dinosaurs roaming through this alpine tundra, grazing on the lichen and downy vegetation.

At that moment, I so wanted to keep riding up the Dempster; the temptation, almost irresistible, but we weren't prepared for that type of journey and time, unfortunately, didn't allow. Nonetheless, to actually have ridden part way up the Dempster was such a privilege; with that thought, we turned back towards Dawson City.

Sitting on the balcony of the Triple J hotel that evening, we sat drinking wine, playing Uno and chatting about the day. I miss those moments. At a nearby table, a group of Americans sat eating, but mostly drinking. The more inebriated they became, the louder they got, each person competing to be heard. This was better than watching television!

One of the females in the party suddenly shouted to the bartender,

"Hey! Can we have the check?"

Please! I thought silently.

Acknowledging the group, the red-haired bartender walked over to the table handing over the bill, smiling politely.

Squinting at the bill, the woman asked, *"Is that Canadian or American?"*

Our ears pricked up.

"Er, Canadian," the bartender replied pleasantly.

"What's that in real fucking money?" she persisted.

We couldn't believe what we were hearing. Remaining calm and still smiling, however a little more strained, the bartender calculated the bill into American dollars.

Once the group had gone, we got chatting to the bar-tender about what had happened.

"That happens quite a lot," he explained.

"But, this is Canada. Does that mean that you can pay in Alaska in Canadian dollars?" I asked.

"Hell, no," he laughed.

As a Scot; this hit home somewhat. How many times have we been referred to as English or the UK being called England? Whilst working for the military in Germany, a colleague asked me when I was going back to England.

"I'm going back to Scotland, not England," I replied.

"Oh, you know what I mean?" she continued.

I left it without saying anything, but can you imagine if I had asked her when she was going back to Scotland?

So relaxed was the D2D, you could turn up at anytime over the two days and take part or just watch the goings on. We had decided to attend the evening gatherings and explore more of Dawson during the day.

Taking an inflatable boat, steered by a wiry, older man, we paddled down the Klondike River which flowed into the Yukon. As we floated on the current, the guide pointed out the bald eagles perched in the trees and where there were beaver dams.

As the rapids swept us around a bend in the river, there on the bank below a steep cliff, a moose calf lay watching us float by.

Seeing no mum with the calf, I frantically cried, *"oh no, we've got to help it!"*
There wasn't time to do anything as the current was too strong to stop at the bank.

Mike, ever the logical person, replied, *"There's nothing we can do Lynn,"*
I could see the guide thinking about the situation, *"the mum could be around somewhere, but it kinda looks like the calf may have slipped down the embankment."*

"The calf looks healthy, so he has a fighting chance," he continued.

I felt powerless to help the baby moose and the guide, seeing me upset, waited until we were in calmer waters, took out his mobile phone and called an animal welfare line. Reporting the calf and its location. I could see from the guide's face that it wasn't good news. When he came off the phone, he shook his head, *"they're so busy at the moment. I don't think they'll manage to do anything about the calf."*

Picking up the paddle, he continued, *"The mum could be near. The calf isn't distressed."*

I looked at him, *"thank you for trying. You're right; it looked like it was chilling out. And, I guess, it's nature if it doesn't make it."*

I still felt so sad, but this is a wild and tough country, and only the strong will survive. I kept telling myself that the mum would find her baby!

We were cramming so much into our stay in Dawson; next on the agenda, a trip on the ferry back over the Yukon to the Sternwheelers Graveyard. Parking the bikes, we walked along the banks of the Yukon until we came across the Sternwheelers, also known as Paddle Steamers. In their heyday, especially during the Gold Rush, the Sternwheelers ruled the rivers. The gradual demise of these magnificent boats came as a result of roads.

Now, lying on the banks of the Yukon, nature is taking, for its own, what we've cast away. The once, majestic river boats, now a ramshackle of wood and rusty metal with plants using the structures to grow and weave up and around. And all around, spruce trees swaying in the breeze.

Mike couldn't resist climbing on every wooden paddle or rusty part he could find! I watched from the ground, telling him to be careful; I wouldn't be following Mike in climbing all over the ruins. Although respectful of the history of the Sternwheelers, I don't like rusty, old things; they freak me out!

While Mike clambered all over the rickety structures, I was fighting off the mosquitoes, arms flapping.

Eventually having seen enough, Mike climbed down and we started the walk back along the waterfront to the bikes. The ground was rocky and unstable, causing Mike to stumble and jar his knee. Wincing at the pain, he had to lean on me for support all the way back to his bike. *Would Mike be fit to ride?* I thought; but once back on his bike, I knew that he was.

By the time we had ridden back onto the ferry, the heat of the day was giving way to gathering thundery clouds rolling in. The air was heavy with the musky smell of the impending storm. On the ferry, crossing the Yukon, were around 20 other bikers, all looking up at the darkening skies. *They must be heading to D2D,* I guessed. *Would we get back to camp before the storm hit?*

My answer came as we rode off the ferry; a deluge of water fell from the heavy, black clouds and, in seconds, we were soaked to the skin. Reaching the campsite, all we could do was quickly park the bikes quickly dive into the tent, wet clothes and all!

From the shelter of the tent, we watched torrents of water running down the unpaved roads; the sound of rain against the tent, almost deafening.

As quickly as it had started, the rain stopped, the storm had blown over; or so we thought. During the night, the pitter-patter of raindrops briefly woke us up. That warm, cosy, safe feeling washed over me, lying in my sleeping bag while the rain fell outside, lulling me back to sleep.

It was still raining when we woke up, not as heavy, but didn't let up until nearly lunchtime. The plan had been to take part in the D2D Poker Run; 60 miles of adventure riding through the historic Gold Rush fields. Looking out of the tent, we hummed and hawed whether to go or not. The roads would be slippery & treacherous and these would be dirt roads. With our own bikes, I wouldn't have minded but with rentals, it really wasn't worth the risk. Having weighed up the 'What if's', we knew that it would be best to pass on the Poker Run.

Instead, I went for a hike, exploring the trails above Dawson City, all the while, listening out for bears.

By the time I had returned to the tent, the sun was beating down and the roads already baked dry. *Had it actually rained at all?* At home in Scotland, that amount of rain would have turned the ground muddy for quite a while. The soil in Alaska, seems to be very sandy and almost grey, whereas Scottish soil is brown and, sometimes, black due to the peat.

Closing my eyes, I soaked up the warmth of the sun's rays. *Shit! Sun cream!* I thought, remembering my Celtic skin! With the appropriate Factor 50+ covering every bit of visible skin, there was still time before D2D but not long enough to go far afield.

A ride up to Midnight Dome Viewpoint, looking over Dawson City, was a good small jaunt. The gentle winding road took us up to a vantage point overlooking the Yukon River far below, and the Klondike valleys. We weren't the only folk enjoying the view; I noticed a few other bikers from the campsite.

Saying hi to our fellow riders, I noticed the couple who were camped next to us. I had a feeling that they were father and daughter.

"Did you ride up the easy way?" asked the daughter.

I don't like you, I thought.

"Well, we came up the road way," I answered smiling politely.

"We came straight up the dirt track. Why have off road bikes and not use them properly?" she added.

Smiling, I thought, *I really don't like you.*

I heard her father whisper to her, *"you can't say things like that."*

Oh, to be young, judgemental, obnoxious and gobby!

Heading back down the 'easy way', it was time to get ready for D2D.

The annual meeting turned out to be an extremely relaxed gathering of like-minded people; motorcycle enthusiasts. The main event of the evening was a BBQ and time to catch up with old pals over a beer, or welcome new friends to the D2D family. It wasn't long before we were chatting to people from all over Canada and the States.

There didn't seem to be any rigid schedule to any of the events; people seemed to drift from the BBQ to their bikes to take part in the street games.

I was tempted to have a go at the games, but, again, if it had been my own bike, I wouldn't have hesitated. With our rentals safely parked by the tent, we opted to watch the goings on from the steps outside the Triple J Hotel.

The first of the games was to blindfold the rider who then has to ride their motorbike slowly and stop as close as possible to the target on the road; no peeking allowed and, without riding into the onlookers! Other games that followed were just as crazy, but so much fun!

D2D carried on until midnight and it was still daylight; this was the summer solstice and being in the northern hemisphere, almost 24 hours daylight. Actually, officially it's 21.5 hours of daylight. At around 2am, the sun kind of dips below the horizon but it's still light, an eerie glow in the skies, and then, the sun appears again for another 21.5 hours. I wondered if I would be able to sleep while it was still daylight; yep, no problem.

The flip side of the long days is when winter comes; only four hours of daylight at the winter solstice. It takes a special type of person, I think, to be able to cope with these extremes; I know that I wouldn't want to.

During our lifetime, there are places we visit, whether it's a journey of discovery on bikes, or somewhere we call home; that have a lasting impact on us. Dawson City was one of those places and now, it was time to leave. With a slight tinge of sadness, we rode out of Dawson City; sad but at the same time, happy to have had the opportunity to experience this original and vibrant little city. We may never return to Dawson City and, if we don't, that's fine; we have our memories and there are so many other places in the world to discover.

Our journey from Dawson city was south on the Klondike Highway towards Whitehorse; but with six hours of riding to get there, we had planned to stop halfway for the night. Checking the map, the small town of Carmacks was just over halfway; perfect. The name, Carmacks, seemed familiar; *have we been here already?* We've visited or passed through so many places that we're now forgetting where we've been and places we've perhaps just seen signposts for.

Then it came to me; it sounds like the Scottish confectionery, Caramac!

Sweeties aside, named after George Carmacks, one of the first people to discover gold in the Klondike, the town of Carmacks is in a prime location for travelling by river or road. Also known as the *hub of the Yukon*, Carmacks is home to the *Little Salmon* First Nation and has been a favourite hunting and fishing area long before the Gold Rush.

The freedom of this journey meant that plans can and do change; today, the 23rd June, was one of those days. Having stopped briefly in Pelly Crossing for a bite to eat, Mike's phone rang; it was our son, Daryl. Standing in the sun by the bikes, I knew that it was wonderful news Mike was hearing. Straining to get my ear near the phone, I tried my best to listen in. Mike was beaming; realising that I couldn't quite hear, Mike was repeating what he was being told.

"*A girl, yes. Healthy. Mum's doing well, brilliant! A good weight; wow, dark hair! Imogen Marie; that's a lovely name. Immi, for short; fantastic!*"

By this time, I was jumping for joy, around Mike and the bikes.

We would be going back home to a new granddaughter, Imogen Marie Aitken!

"*Your mum wants to chat with you Daryl; love you all,*" Mike said, handing me the phone.

I chatted with Daryl for a few minutes, just happy to hear

that everyone was well and told him that I loved them all.

The call over, we hugged each other, jumping for joy.

"How do you fancy going straight to Whitehorse?" Mike suggested.

"Definitely," I replied, still smiling *"at least we'll get wifi and better reception."*

Apparently, happiness releases endorphins; I'm sure that's true as the wonderful news of wee Imogen's arrival in the world, gave us a boost of energy to push on for another 280 Km to Whitehorse. Riding along, the feeling of warmth, happiness and love enveloped me; I could hardly wait to meet our new granddaughter.

It's been over two years since we were last in Whitehorse. Riding into town today, the 23rd June, was a happy day and yet, memories of two years ago came flooding back. Then, it had been a journey to get back to our daughter, Hazel, as quickly as possible.

Two years ago, our hearts were heavy with worry for Hazel and the distance was so great to get back to her. But, you know what?

Hazel is an amazing young lady; strong, beautiful and successful. No, those worries are in the past, and that's where they'll remain.

Arriving at a budget, basic but comfy hotel, we checked in and lugged our kit from the bikes into the room. I don't know why, but I always look at the pillows, hoping that there will be a chocolate sitting there. Nope, no chocolate.

In the tent, there's a place for everything, but that goes out the window whenever we stay in a hotel. Instead of order and harmony, there was an explosion of clothes around the room as we set about getting ready to go out for a meal and a few celebratory drinks.

It's a human trait to want to share good news with friends and family, and at home, that's exactly what I would have been doing. I was on cloud nine about our new granddaughter; I wanted to shout the good news from the rooftops. But, there was no-one here to tell, so I did the next best thing, or so I thought. Before going out for a meal, I logged onto the hotel wifi and announced, on Facebook, to my few friends that I was a granny again.

Little did I know that, back home, Daryl hadn't yet gotten around to telling everyone! Oh, shit!

Before breakfast the following morning, I logged onto Facebook to find a message from Daryl.

"Mum, can you stop posting on Facebook? Kim wanted to wait."

To say I felt awful was an understatement. I'm a great believer in saying sorry when I have said or done something to upset someone. I messaged Daryl straightaway apologising to him and to Kim and asking them to forgive me; my emotions had got the better of me.

My stomach was churning while I waited for an answer. It wasn't long before Daryl typed back.

"It's okay Mum. Of course you're forgiven. And, I know that you were just excited about your second granddaughter."

Daryl's message helped me feel slightly better, but I wanted to say sorry over the phone. After finding a place for breakfast, I called Daryl.

"Daryl, I'm so sorry. I didn't mean to upset you or Kim; I was so happy, I wasn't thinking clearly."

"Hi Kim. I'm so so sorry! I'm an idiot; I was just so happy!" I pleaded.

There was a slight pause, *"Apology accepted,"* Kim said softly.

"Thank you so much. I feel awful about it. I've only got a few friends on Facebook though."

"You being billy-no-mates is no excuse!" she laughed.

"When we see you, I'll buy you a big box of chocolates," I added.

"Er, I expect a huge box of chocolates Lynn!"

I agreed with those terms and continued to ask how Kim was feeling and how wee Imogen was. There was also Dharyl;

how did she like having a little sister?

"*Dharyl's in awe of Immi,*" Kim said happily.

Having said our goodbyes, I managed to eat some breakfast, feeling happier that I had righted my mistake by saying sorry and a promise to buy Kim the biggest box of chocolates I could find!

Over breakfast, we also chatted about our next move after Whitehorse. Our trip plan was to head towards Haines Junction, onto Beaver Creek, Glenallen and back to Anchorage on Saturday 30th June. Moto Quest was expecting the bikes back on the Saturday. Our last three days would be exploring Anchorage before flying home.

"*Anchorage is just another city. Why don't we call Moto Quest and see if we can hire the bikes for another couple of days?*" I suggested.

Mike thought about it for a few minutes, "*but, where would we go?*" he asked.

"*This is Alaska! We most probably won't be back. Let's make the most of the time we have here,*" I urged.

With a sigh but smiling, Mike pulled out the map from his bag.

"*Let's have a look at the map. We may also not be able to keep the bikes for extra days; someone else might be renting them,*"

Ever the optimist, not!

Pointing to Valdez, Mike said, "*We could ride there; it's meant to be a spectacular road into Valdez.*"

The next call we would make was to Moto Quest and, hopefully rent the bikes for the extra days.

I stood by Mike, waiting patiently. He was smiling so it had to be good news.

"*That's it done,*" he said, putting his phone away, "*We've got the bikes until Sunday evening; we're going to Valdez!*"

I love that part of a trip like this; the open road, to go wherever you fancy.

It was nice to be back in Whitehorse; crisp and clean is how I remembered the town from our first time there. Although warmer this time around, the air was still crisp and clean; Whitehorse has freshness about it.

There, moored on the Yukon River, the *S.S. Klondike* Sternwheeler was as I remembered her; looking the grand lady she still is to this day. Last time, we weren't able to take a tour of her as it was still too early in the season. This time, we wouldn't be disappointed and booked ourselves on a tour of the S.S. *Klondike*. Today's vessel is actually the *Klondike II*; the first sternwheeler ran aground in 1936. Salvaging the machinery and some of the structure, the *S.S. Klondike II* was launched in 1937 and recommenced the Whitehorse-Dawson run, carrying cargo and passengers.

The construction of the Mayo Road brought about the end of transporting freight by river and so, in 1955, the *Klondike II* sailed into Whitehorse for the last time.

Now, a National Historic Site and beautifully restored, The *Klondike II* was opened to the public in 1981. The tour guide taking us around the sternwheeler took us back to bygone days when the *S.S. Klondike* and other sternwheelers ruled the rivers.

Mike and I both know when it's time to move on, and as nice as Whitehorse is, we were ready to leave, excited about the next part of the journey. Being the last night in Whitehorse, we thought we would try somewhere local, where the townsfolk frequent. After dinner, Mike pointed to the 98' Breakfast Club, a rundown looking place.

I wasn't sure but agreed to give it a go. However, as soon as I walked in, I knew that I wouldn't like it here.

"Let's have one drink here; you never know," Mike said on seeing my frown.

Nodding, I followed him to the bar.

"Howdy there folks! What can I get you?" the friendly bartender smiled.

Maybe I was wrong about the place.

"Do you have wine?" I asked.

"Wine, did you say?" he replied.

"*No, maam, that's something we don't have.*"

Nope! I wasn't wrong! I thought, smiling. "*Um, I'll just have a beer, just beer.*"

With our beers, we sat at a sticky, round wooden table.

"*Cheers!*" we both said, clinking bottles.

"*Beer's not bad,*" I said, smiling.

Actually, the beer wasn't too bad at all; the local drunk, on the other hand, was just too much to bear.

We must have looked like newbies as, like a mosquito to fresh new blood, she was there! I'm the type of person who can get on a bus, and be the unlucky one the drunk is going to sit near or, heaven forbid, beside! Loud, brash, almost falling over, we were fresh victims for her.

I've never drank a bottle of beer so quickly!

"*Right! That's it, let's go!*" I said, grabbing my bag.

"*Yep!*" Mike agreed, following me out of the joint.

"*OK, we've done local; let's find somewhere with nice seats and wine!*" I said, at the same time, laughing.

The next morning, with the sun shining, we rode out of Whitehorse on the next leg of our journey. We were now on the same roads we had ridden two years ago. Passing the Robert Service Campsite, I briefly glanced to the left.

That was where we stayed last time we were in Whitehorse, I thought.

Robert Service was known as the *Bard of the Yukon;* one of his most famous poems being, 'The Cremation of Sam McGee'.

It wasn't long before Whitehorse was far behind us and we were back in the wilderness.

I had a momentary tinge of sadness, knowing that we only had a week left before going home. The sadness passed quickly because we were going back to our family and would meet our new granddaughter. As we rode into a small town for lunch, (I wish I could remember the name of the place!) the air was filled with tiny, white tufts of cottonwood seeds blowing in the warm breeze. Like fluffy clouds on the breeze, they reminded me of dandelion seeds, when you blow the heads, reciting, '*he loves me, he loves me not*'.

Parking the bikes, I took my helmet off, only to get a face full of cottonwood. Spitting them out and wiping them away from my eyes, I still admired the spectacle.

The small cafe we went into, was quiet; just us at one table and three local folk at another. It wasn't too long before we exchanged pleasantries.

I asked about the cottonwood seeds; I wasn't completely sure that's what they were.

"*They sure are. It's that time of year when the release their seeds,*" one of the men confirmed.

"*It's lovely,*" I said

"*Not if you're wanting to paint yer house, it ain't,*" he came right back at me.

"*Hmm, I'd not thought of that,*" I replied, with an image in my head of a freshly painted house, covered in cottonwood seeds!

Fed and watered, we donned our helmets whilst still in the cafe. I didn't really want to be spitting out cottonwood again!

The long days of which we didn't experience the first time we were here, brought with it, not only sunlight and warmth, but a wealth of flowers and plants.

On either side of the road, there were masses of small, purple flowers; their growing season a brief moment in time to capture as many nutrients from the extended sunny days, before the long and harsh winter returns, forcing them to sleep beneath the deep snow and ice.

My thoughts of the nature around us were interrupted as I noticed a car coming towards us on our side of the road.

"*What the hell?*" I shouted to myself, whilst finding a safe part of the road, out of this idiot's way.

Mike had taken the same action, but not without flapping his arm at the driver.

The driver veered back towards his side of the road but still close enough to me that I caught the strong whiff of weed coming from the open window. He was as high as a kite, or driving while buzzed, as they call it in the States.

Each time, an incident happens when I'm riding, I'm always thankful that I sat my Advanced Rider's test. Following this, I feel that I have an 'invisible bubble' around me; I can see situations before they happen; I'm aware of the environment that I'm riding through. It could be something as simple as noticing the bins outside ready for emptying.

Would I ride around the next bend and find a bin lorry blocking the road?

Out for a ride back home, I followed behind a van with a pharmacist's name on it; I knew that the next village had that same pharmacy. *I think he might be signalling soon to pull over at the pharmacy,* I thought. And sure enough, he did.

If any of our children decided to ride a motorcycle, I wouldn't try to stop them; it's fun and can be safe. But, I will urge them to carry on with their training even after passing their basic licence.

Back in Alaska, claiming our side of the road again, we rode on until we reached Skagway. This is where we would be taking a ferry to Haines.

The ferry wasn't due to leave for another few hours, giving us time to have a look around Skagway.

Once a quaint, picturesque little town and, not unlike Dawson City, the location of Skagway has brought the tourists in via cruise liners. Rumour has it that some of the shops in Skagway, are owned by the cruise companies; K-ching! There's either the touristy (made in China) shops, or expensive jewellery and fur shops all waiting for the next lot of visitors and their cash.

I would imagine that, during the winter when the water is frozen and the tourists aren't there, Skagway goes back to being the small, quaint town it once was.

To the Native Americans, Skagua (Skagway) meaning windy place, was a fishing and hunting area.

The Skagway today wasn't for us, but it was still too early

for the ferry. Again, Mike had done his homework and knew of a short ride of interest ten miles out of Skagway.

This was the start of the famous Chilkoot Pass, where hopeful prospectors began the dangerous trek in search for gold. Riding by the start of the Pass, we didn't stop but kept going further on around a lake to another historic site which Mike had read about; Dyea. Parking the bikes, we walked around what was the boomtown of Dyea; difficult to imagine this being anything other than countryside. Mother Nature reclaiming the land for herself. The demise of Dyea came about as a result of the railroad; and so, Skagway flourished whilst Dyea died.

Close by is Slide Cemetery; there are not many graveyards where the people all died on the exact same day and at the same time.

The name, Slide Cemetery, is a clue to the reason why. On 3rd April, 1898 (Palm Sunday), an avalanche swept down from the mountains and killed over 60 stampeders, burying them under a mass of snow; their quest for gold abruptly came to an end.

The potential risk of an avalanche had been forewarned by the locals, and those who died took the fatal decision to ignore the advice. Strolling around the cemetery, we read every gravestone, wondering what each person would have been like. Whatever their background, they were all here for the same reason; gold. *How many families were left with no husband or father?* I wondered

To lift our spirits after the sadness of the cemetery, we rode on further across a small wooden bridge and started up a dirt rocky track. Dirt tracks, to me scream out, FUN! And this one was no different. Following Mike, we continued up and up, avoiding large rocks; I knew that Mike was enjoying this as much as me. I could hear the smaller stones hitting off the metal bash plate underneath my bike.

The track started getting a little bit more challenging which, on our own bikes and not fully loaded, would've been even more fun; however, these were rentals and we were always mindful that the bikes had to be handed back in a few days.

Mike stopped up ahead, lifting his visor. I pulled up just behind him. *"It's tempting, Mike, but they're not our bikes. I think we should turn back,"* I called to him.

"Yep, you're right. It was fun though!" he agreed, smiling.

Riding carefully back down the dirt track, we were, once more, on the road to Skagway. Arriving back into the hustle and bustle of Skagway, I was glad that we had explored further field; and, we were still in good time for the ferry.

I knew nothing about the ferry we were going on, other than our journey would take a couple of hours to reach Haines.

Sitting in the queue, we soon realised that the vehicles waiting to board, all had different destinations on their dashboards. *I wonder how long it takes to get to these other stops?*

When the ferry parking attendant came to check our tickets, I had to ask him about the ferry's journey.

"A week," he replied.

Looking in amazement from the attendant to the small, basic looking ferry, I asked, *"a week? On that?"*

The man nodded, smiling at my reaction.

"It's really the only way to transport folk and their vehicles around here. It's a vital service," he explained.

I discovered later that the ferry service, the Alaska Marine Highway, is operated by the State of Alaska and truly is a lifeline to tiny, remote communities.

Maybe, the ferry will be nicer onboard than from the first impression it gave me, I thought.

On boarding the ferry, there were no hidden surprises; it was a basic as they come. We were thankful that it was just a two hour journey for us.

"There's a TV room," Mike said, pointing to the plan of the ferry.

Wandering down to the room, the makeshift chairs were pointing towards a tiny television in a shabby, looking room.

"Well, it did say a television room," I shrugged.

Not bothering with the television, we went, instead, to look out of the windows, the view was spectacular; not unlike Norway and the fjords. Outside, on the sundeck, the views were even more breathtaking; this was Norway on steroids!

The air was cool, but refreshing at the same time. On the deck were mostly young people, some swinging in hammocks and others setting up their tents, all preparing themselves for a week on this vessel. Thinking back to when we lived in Germany and the DFDS ferries we travelled to and from the continent; they were plush compared to this.

Two hours later and we were docking in Haines. Mike, haven been a sailor, loves to watch the whole docking procedure; usually giving me a running commentary of what's happening at the same time.

As we rode off the ferry into Haines, I felt sorry for the passengers staying on the vessel for a week!

Tonight in Haines, we were booked into a hotel overlooking the bay. The following morning before leaving, downtown is where we headed for breakfast and a wander around the shops.

Talking to shop owners, it was evident that Haines has managed to escape the commercialism that has befallen Skagway; and yet, the small independent shops here have managed to get by on the small tourist trade that visits or passes through Haines.

Leaving Haines, there was 148 miles of riding to reach our next destination, Haines Junction; 148 miles of stunning scenery and a great road for biking, albeit cold. An icy wind blew down from the hills; I was glad that I had put on an extra layer that morning.

Stopping for a short break, Mike pointed out bear pooh on the road.

"Have you noticed all the bear pooh on the roads?" he asked me. *"Why shit on the road when there's a whole lot of forest?"* he continued.

I replied, '*Well, maybe they've decided to shit on our land because we keep shitting on theirs*'.

"*True, but can you imagine coming around a bend and seeing a grizzly having a dump?*"

I just had to laugh at that image!

Finally, we reached the Wanderer's Inn, a lovely hostel we had stayed at before, but this time we were camping in the garden rather than sleeping inside, and, yet still able to use their facilities.

I recognised Martin, the Inn owner straightaway and, just like the first time here, Martin greeted us warmly. Haines Junction is, as the name suggests, at a junction, a crossroads and surrounded by beautiful mountains, rugged and wild. The icy wind we had experienced riding towards Haines Junction was gone and it was feeling like summer again; we were in a suntrap.

Once our tent was set up, Mike and I headed indoors to make our dinner, making full use of the kitchen facilities. Already eating his meal at the table was another visitor staying overnight. The man was a retired professor visiting his daughter who was working in the parks. As ever, we struck up a conversation with him and the Inn owner. It turned out the retired professor was an expert on wilderness management, and an interesting conversation followed suit. I had to ask him how he felt about the reintroduction of wolves in countries such as Scotland and, coming from an expert, he was totally in favour of it.

I was glad to hear this as I'm also in favour of bringing the wolves back; it's the farmers who are against it! I recently watched a programme where they had reintroduced wolves into Yellowstone National Park.

The natural order of the park has been restored, all because of the wolves.

Our friend, Kathy once said, "*Everything fits together in nature, except us. We're aliens on this planet.*" I completely agree with her.

That evening, in the Wanderer's Inn, we were joined by another visitor who passed around cider and joined the chat.

After talking about the extended summer daylight hours, Martin said, *"Parents here don't tell their kids to come back when it's getting dark cos they'll be out until August!"*

I could just imagine children playing outside, thinking, *Wow! I'm tired, but it's not dark yet; let's play some more!*

After saying our goodbyes, we settled into our sleeping bags for the night; it's nice going to sleep having spent a pleasant evening.

The next morning was bright and sunny, but with a chill in the air; it would soon warm up.

Leaving Wanderer's Inn, we both knew that we wouldn't be back; not that we didn't like Haines Junction, we did, but life is brief and the world, huge.

Riding along, ever watchful for wildlife; I saw Mike glancing to the right and then looking again, while pulling over.

Instinctively, I knew that he had spotted something; Passing Mike, I signalled to the right and rode a bit further down the road and onto the hard shoulder. Mike was already off his bike and looking over to a lush meadow.

There was no point riding back to where Mike had parked; it was only a short walk back. This is when I was injured by a grizzly; not what you're thinking!

Seeing what Mike had spotted, a grizzly, excitement got the better of me and I started running. Tripping over what I think was my own foot, I found myself cycling in the air, trying to stay upright; hitting the gravel with my bare hands; *Ouch!*

Picking myself up, I walked up to Mike, who had been so busy watching the bear, that he hadn't seen me fall. Turning to look at me, he saw both my hands had been skinned after hitting the gravel, blood pouring out.

"What the hell did you do?" he asked.

When I told him, he said that, technically, I had been injured by a grizzly. I don't think me falling over myself counts.

Watching the bear from a safe distance, he was a sight to behold; majestic and cuddly.......did I just call this massive beast 'cuddly?' *I wonder if he/she can smell my blood?* I thought. The bear wasn't sniffing the air, a good sign; it was too busy sitting in the meadow, eating flowers and enjoying the warmth of the sun. Needless to say, we had the bear spray to hand, just in case.

Incredibly, the bear wasn't bothered about us or going anywhere; we could have stayed longer and, as tempting as that was, we had to get going. Back at the bikes, Mike looked out the first aid kit, picked the gravel out of my hands and patched me up.

Retracing our steps from the first trip, we headed for Beaver Creek and Buckshot Betty's. Beaver Creek was where we had turned back and made the long journey back home when Hazel needed us. Now, we were going back. *I wonder if we'll see Buckshot Betty?*

Buckshot Betty suits her nickname; a small lady and, yet, a force of nature. I remember her being nice, kind and slightly scary at the same time.

Today's ride was only 181 miles; a perfect distance for being able to stop if we wanted to see something and not having to merely eat up the miles to get to Beaver Creek.

Arriving in Beaver Creek, and it was just as I remembered it except, this time, the weather was hot. Remembering our first time, it was so cold that we had decided to stay in one of the rooms; Betty was kind enough to give us a plush suite at half the price. Tonight, we would be camping.

Climbing the wooden steps into Buckshot Betty's, we waited to check in.

We heard Betty before we saw her, and then, there she was,

"I'll be right there folks!" she called us while pouring coffee for a customer.

Betty was serving in the restaurant, hobbling around with a cast on her leg. I swear, I have never seen someone with a cast, move so quickly!

"Hey, folks! What can I do for you today?" she said, pen in hand.

"Hi, we'd like to book a tent site for the night please?"

"Sure thing," she drawled.

"And, can we book a table for dinner here this evening please?" I asked.

"No problem," Betty answered.

After paying, she was off again like a whirlwind serving customers; it was nice to see her again.

What a change the campsite behind Buckshot Betty's was compared to the first time we were here; the summer weather always makes places look more inviting, I think.
Tent up and bikes parked right beside us; we were ready for dinner.

Going into the restaurant, we were glad that we had reserved a table; it was fairly busy. *Where did all these people come from?* I wondered. I'm sure Beaver Creek exists because of passing trade; people driving through en-route to other destinations.

I can't see Beaver Creek being a holiday destination; more of a '*let's stop for a break and grab a bite to eat,*' sort of place.

Sitting at our table, we watched Betty whizzing around serving customers; her voice carried around the restaurant. Soon, Betty was by us, taking our order. There wasn't much on the menu for vegetarians, "*I'm vegetarian, so I'll have a ranch salad and fries,*" I asked.

Mike ordered his food and she was gone just as Mike said "*please.*"

It wasn't long before our food was ready and Betty brought it to the table. Putting my glasses on, I noticed my salad had ham on it.

Getting Betty's attention, she hobbled to our table.

"*I'm sorry Betty, but I'm vegetarian and my salad has ham on it,*" I said quietly, hating to make a fuss.

Loudly, Betty answered, "*Ranch salad has ham on it, everyone knows that!*"

Aw, shit. Now people are looking at us.

"*I'm sorry, but I didn't know that. I'm a vegetarian, I don't eat meat,*" I answered, embarrassed.

"*Well, you should've said!*" she replied, starting to walk away.

Now, Betty had pushed the wrong button! Politely, I called after her, "*I did say!*" and, *under my breath,* "*if you'd only listened!*" Well, I didn't want her spitting into my food. And I remembered that this lady had survived a bear chasing her!

Maybe, Betty was in pain with her leg, or having a bad day, but that's no excuse for rudeness, especially in hospitality. So, if you're going through Beaver Creek, you might see the nice Betty, or you'll be greeted by the Tasmanian Devil! Flip a coin and take your chances!

The following day, we said goodbye to Beaver Creek and Buckshot Betty's; we won't be back!

It was only 20 miles and we were back in Alaska; the ride today was a fairly long one, 248 miles to Glenallen, via Tok.

VALDEZ. MOUNTAINS, CASCADING WATERFALLS AND OIL!

Glenallen was another crossroads town, where, originally, we had planned to stay the night. Stopping to fuel up, I asked, *"how far is it to Valdez?"*

Mike knew why I was asking. *"You want to keep going?"* he asked.

"Depending on the distance, yes, why not?"

There wasn't much in Glenallen and I would rather go somewhere interesting, especially since time was running out on this trip. We would be back on the plane, heading home before we knew it.

Looking at the map, it was only an extra two hour ride to Valdez; we could do that. Decision made, we would keep going and spend an extra night in Valdez. Fully fuelled and having stopped for a coffee, we were ready for the next stage to Valdez.

Some sections of the road were 55 Mph zones, and yet, 18 wheeler trucks were hurtling past us doing about 80; keeping to the speed limit, we were the slowest vehicles on the road!

It was almost dangerous going this slow, so we sped up slightly, although it just didn't feel right.

The road down through Thompson Pass to Valdez was as spectacular as we had been told; waterfalls on either side of the road and glaciers. I was glad we had decided to keep the bikes longer; after hearing how spectacular the ride was and missing it, would have been sad.

Above us, bald eagles soared high, effortless, on thermals. The beautiful bird should have a nicer name; it's not bald, but has white feathers. The white headed eagle would be a kinder name.

While eagles soared, we *surfed* the frost heaves; bumps in the road due to the change of temperature in the permafrost beneath us. I felt free; it was exhilarating.

Although, it had been a long ride, the views and the road had been so much fun, the time had flown by. Riding into Valdez, and now I was aware of my backside complaining; I would be glad to get off my bike and stretch.

Finding the campsite, we noticed that there were all RVs; *I hope it's not one of these RV only campsites,* I thought.

In the reception, however, the lady explained that there was a separate area for tents; *that's a relief!*

After checking in, we rode our bikes to the tenting area, a bit further down the road. Parking our bikes, I couldn't see any tent sites, just a wooded hill which turned out to be where we could camp. We could choose any free site, the receptionist had informed us.

Climbing wooden steps up through the trees, we soon realised how the set up was; on each level part of the hill was a wooden decking tent site.

Stopping at each level, I said, *"oh, this is nice, Mike. What about here?"*

"Let's keep going up," Mike said.

As we climbed higher, we started noticing bunnies, not wild rabbits, but like pet bunnies. *Strange,* I thought.

Reaching the top of the hill and crossing a tiny wooden

bridge, we found ourselves at the top of the hill, above the trees, looking out over Valdez.

We couldn't believe our luck, the site was empty; we were claiming the 'penthouse suite' for our own! There was even decking; this was plush.

Situated on the north shore of Port Valdez, Valdez reminded me of a quaint, coastal fishing village surrounded by mountains.

Tent up. Time for a much needed bite to eat and a wander around town.

Climbing down from our penthouse suite, we saw more multi-coloured rabbits; I was going to have to find out about them. The bunnies weren't just restricted to the wooded hill; they seemed to be all around town wherever there was grass. Chatting to the receptionist who checked us in, she told us that some years ago, a domestic rabbit had escaped or been released and simply did what rabbits do!

You know when a name is familiar, but you just can't place it? That's how I felt about Valdez, but a trip to the museum, and the penny dropped; the Exxon Valdez oil spill disaster in 1989. The oil tanker, Exxon Valdez ran aground on Bligh Reef, spilling 11 million gallons of crude oil into the Prince William Sound. The impact on the wildlife was disastrous and an enormous clean up was undertaken but not before hundreds of thousands of animals died.

Looking out to the seemingly idyllic Sound, it's hard to imagine that still to this day; the environmental impact is being felt. The Killer Whale populations haven't yet recovered and fish such as herring have not returned; will they ever? To look over to the oil storage tanks on the far side of the bay, I wonder if there's a protection plan for a natural disaster such as an earthquake.

Our last night in Valdez; we wouldn't be going out to eat; instead, I was going to cook on our decking outside our penthouse suite! Dinner was planned and, as there was a fire pit, Mike had bought the firewood from the supermarket; he was the Feuermeister.

I started looking out the pots and food, ready to cook our meal, while Mike lit the fire. From the fire pit, I could hear Mike striking matches and muttering. I kind of guessed that he was having difficulty lighting the fire; looking over at the smoke and no flames confirmed this.

"*Goddamned firewood!,*" he muttered louder.

"*Er, how's it going?*" I asked.

Mike stood up, emerging out of the smoke, coughing, "*what **do you** think?*"

That was my cue to just stay quiet and let him get on with it.

To my horror, out came the can of oil lubricant; "*this'll do it,*" Mike said, squirting oil into the pit.

A few flames appeared and died, replaced by even more smoke; there was no way I was going to start cooking until Mike got control of the fire!

Sitting in the tent, away from the smoke, I knew that there wasn't much oil lubricant in the can; he would just have to give up trying and accept the fact that the firewood was too damp or unseasoned and we wouldn't be having a fire tonight.

No, not Mike; this was not going to beat him! Piercing the empty can, he tossed it into the smouldering wood!

That's it! I thought, *I can't stand this any longer.*

When Mike gets this frustrated, there's no point in talking to him, so I walked right past him and across the bridge, "*I'm going to the laundry room!*"

Half an hour of calming myself down, I climbed back up to our site where I found Mike sitting looking glum, a bit like a bah humbug; the fire had beaten him. Instead of a nice crackling fire, there were the remnants of charred wood and blackened, empty oil can.

With a half smile, Mike said, "*we're eating downtown tonight.*"

The next morning, the sky was overcast; hopefully we would get the tent packed up before it started raining.

Working in unison, we, each set about our own tasks. Hearing footsteps coming across the bridge, we both looked up to see the camp ranger approaching us.

"*Hi folks, how're ye all doing?*"

"*Great; just packing up to leave,*" I replied.

He was obviously not in a hurry as he started chatting.

"*No luck with the fire?*" he asked, pointing to the charred wood; we had already binned the can, thank goodness!

Oooh! Touchy subject! I thought.

After telling him where we got the wood and the cost of it, he told us that we could have bought excellent firewood from the camp store for a fraction of the price; not what Mike wanted to hear!

Managing to pack everything on the bikes just as it started to rain; waterproofs donned, we rode out of Valdez.

The rain was now coming down hard, bringing with it, the cold air. Climbing elevation, I started to shiver.

Thankfully, the further we rode, the weather started to improve; the rain stopped and the sun broke out from behind the clouds. Like a chameleon, my body soaked up the warmth of the sun and I wasn't tensing up so much.

Our last evening camping in the wilderness, was at the Matanuska Glacier Recreation State Park situated near the Glacier itself.

Before heading to the campsite, we stopped for a coffee at the Long Rifle Lodge on the Glenn Highway. Sitting at a window table, the views of Matanuska Glacier were magnificent and alluring; 26 miles of ice which seems to stop abruptly; the end of 'road'.

Gazing in awe at the mass of ice, I said, "*Mike, it's amazing! It just looks like a river of ice!*"

Shaking his head, Mike replied, "*Er, honey; it is a river of ice!*"

With the tent up and Mike having successfully lit the fire, there were mixed emotions; feeling fortunate to have been able to finish what we started over three years ago and happy to be going back home to our family and a new granddaughter. And yet at the same time, sad to be going back to civilisation; Anchorage is a city; too many people and all that entails.

Away from the rat race of modern living, life is simpler; back to basics. I'm thirsty, I need water; I'm hungry, I need food; I'm cold, I need warmth.

The next morning, the day started chilly but with the potential to warm up. This was it; time to leave our wilderness retreat and head back to Anchorage.

The road from Matanuska was a treat; good condition with some gentle twisties. Following Mike around the bends, I was loving the ride. We had only been on the road for less than ten minutes when I noticed Mike pulling over towards the side to park; I guessed he had seen a photo opportunity.

The verge Mike was trying to park on was sandy; riding onto the sand, I saw him skid and almost lose control of the bike. It was deeper sand than we had first thought; our nemesis!

Aw, shit! I thought as I followed him, trying to change course before I went into the sand, but too late. My tyre sunk into the sand; struggling to stay upright, the weight of my bike and luggage was too much and I fell to the side with my bike pinning my foot down.

Mike had managed to stay upright so came running over to help lift the bike off my foot. In doing so, the pedal was trapping my foot even more and moving the weight of the bike onto it.

Finally, bike upright and me free with a sore foot, I had a meltdown moment,

"*I'm sorry, I didn't realise that the sand was that deep,*" Mike explained.

Me, angry that I had dropped my bike, cried, "*I was enjoying the road. Why the hell do we have to stop in stupid places for photos of mountains?*" Taking a breath, I continued,

"*It's not worth it. And, anyway, I've seen enough fucking mountains to last me a lifetime!*

Which actually isn't true? Coming from Scotland, I love the mountains. But that was me just hitting out; I was angrier with myself.

Limping around the bike, I checked for any damage, there was none, thankfully.

"*You OK to continue?*" Mike asked, concerned.

"*Yes, I'll be fine. But, let's go and get a coffee and buy aspirin.*"

Mike knew why I wanted aspirin but didn't say anything. I'm a hypochondriac and in my mind I was worrying that my ankle would be bruised and swollen, then that could lead to DVT (deep vein thrombosis) when we were flying home!

After stopping for a coffee and, yes, aspirin, I felt slightly better; albeit with a throbbing ankle. Not only was my ankle sore, my confidence had been knocked and I knew that we were taking the scenic route over Hatcher Pass. Situated between the towns of Willow and Palmer, Hatcher Pass is a road through the mountains.

Turning towards Hatcher Pass, we were soon climbing; leaving the smooth roads behind, the Pass is gravelly and quite cheeky.

Normally, I like cheeky roads and love a challenge, but the fall earlier had knocked my confidence. Stopping for a breather, Mike asked, "*Do you want to turn back and go the other way?*"

Getting off my bike, I turned my back to him and bent over, "*No, we're keeping going. But first, give me a kick up the arse please?*

Mike was happy to oblige! Getting back on my bike, there was no way I was going to let the nerves get the better of me; bring it on! I loved the rest of the ride over Hatcher Pass; at the bottom, I pulled alongside Mike and we high fived each other. Confidence was back!

After leaving Hatcher Pass, I could hardly believe how quickly we reached Anchorage. This was it; the end of the road and the end of a two part journey. A journey of discovery, not only of places, but of myself; a journey of highs and lows. If it hadn't been for this trip, we would never have met the kindest of folk; we thank everyone we were lucky to meet for their hospitality and friendship.

The last night in Anchorage, Alaska, was spent across from the bike rental and campsite in Gwennies; a perfect way to wrap up an adventure of a lifetime.

What next? Well, that's an easy question to answer; home to our family. All the places we've discovered; nothing compares to the love we have for our family.

The Signpost that inspired an adventure

.

Those long roads

Lynn Aitken

Picnic stop on the Lost Coast

MOTORCYCLE KIT LIST – WHAT WE TOOK

DOCUMENTATION

Passport
Driving Licence
International Driving Permit
Bike insurance
Travel insurance
Bike registration document
Cash
Bank/credit cards
Notebook
Maps/guide books
Accident report form

Photocopies of all docs & scanned back- ups on a robust USB

CAMPING

Tent
Sleeping bag & liner
Sleeping mattress
Air pump
Mozzie head net
Tent light
Air pillow
head torch
Fire lighting steel & flint
Table/chairs (collapsible)
Clothes pegs/paracord
Playing cards/games

COOKING

Camping stove
Fuel bottle
Utensils
Chopping board
Water container
Mug/wine glass (optional!)
Coffee press
Plastic containers
scourer/washing up liquid

COOKING

Cork screw
Tin opener
Condiments
Biodegradable litter bags
Lighter
Camping plate/bowl
Universal sink plug
Food bag clips

CLOTHING

Helmet & pinlock visor
Bike jacket/trousers
Lightweight, quilted jacket
Breathable, waterproof jacket/trousers
Thermal long johns (I wore these in bed!)
Fleece
Lightweight cotton T-shirts (quick drying)
Socks/underwear
Neck buff
Gloves & liners
Bike boots & walking boots
Trousers/shorts

CLOTHING

Flip flops
Swimwear
Trainers/casual shoes
Woolly hat
*Cotton neckerchief for head

PERSONAL STUFF

*Medication
Wash bag
*Lightweight towel
Toiletries

SPARES/TOOLS

Tool kit/multi tool
Puncture repair kit
Tyre pressure gauge
Cable ties/Gaffa tape
Chain lube
*Spare keys
Mini torch
Security chain
Helmet lock

MISCELLANEOUS

Spare batteries
Bum bag
Phone & charger
*Satnav
Earplugs
Sunglasses
Book/E-reader & reading glasses

First Aid kit
Compass
Rucksack
Binoculars
Camera
Small Laptop & charger
Roll bag
Travel clothes washing liquid

Hints & Tips

- Neckerchief for head helps stop the itching
- We kept each other's spare keys
- Order enough medication well in advance
- Maps were more reliable in remote places
- I took a lightweight, holiday beach towel
- Keep clothes at the bottom of sleeping bag; keeps them warm for putting on in the morning
- Calendar/diary; keeps track of where and when

MEXICO

Exploring on foot

Lynn Aitken

Copper Canyon

Lynn Aitken

USA

Lynn Aitken

Rio Grande Village, Big Bend

Lynn Aitken

Lynn Aitken

Keeping cosy!

CANADA

Lynn Aitken

Lynn Aitken

Lynn Aitken

ALASKA (USA)

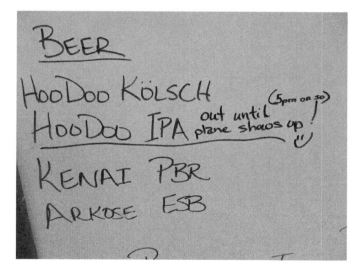

BEER

HooDoo KÖLSCH
HooDoo IPA out until (5pm or so)
plane shows up!

KENAI PBR
ARKOSE ESB

Lynn Aitken

Lynn Aitken

AMERICA'S NATIONAL PARKS

The Parks We Visited

The National Park Service has looked after the national parks since 1916. As well as preserving the history of the First Nation, the Service has protected the fragile ecosystem within the parks.

Wildlife can roam freely without the fear of hunting and humans very much have to 'fit' into the environment.

Big Bend, Texas

This vast park is located in the Chihuahuan Desert. A desert conjures up images of sand and cacti and you'll find this in Big Bend, for sure. However, there's so much more to the park. Bird watchers come from all over to enjoy the 450+ species of birds which call Big Bend their home. The only birds we managed to see were countless Roadrunners. These funny little birds really do run; and fast!

Camping:
There's either *Backcountry* or *Frontcountry* camping to choose from. *Backcountry* is what we did in Pine Canyon. For this, we needed to obtain a permit from the Visitor Centre and be given an alloted spot. *Frontcountry* is camping in one of three developed campgrounds. These are, Chisos Basin, Rio Grande Village and Cottonwood.

Roads:
The main road through Big Bend is paved. There are, however, other roads to take when sightseeing. They include improved dirt roads and, more challenging,primitive dirt roads. Again, the Rangers are the best people to get advice from.

Grand Canyon, Arizona

This must be one of most well known national parks. Grand in name and, indeed, grand in nature. The Colorado River, 1.6 km down in the Canyon, splits the park in two. There's the North and South Rims. I would be silly to try and describe the incredible wonder of the Grand Canyon; it's best to just go and experience it for yourself.

Camping:
The South Rim has three campgrounds: Mather, Trailer Village (for RVs) and Desert View.

The North Rim:
DeMotte, Jacob Lake and North Rim campgrounds.

Backcountry:
Bright Angel (at the bottom of Grand Canyon)
Indian Garden Campground (4.8 miles from the South Rim on the Bright Angel Trail)
Cottonwood (below the North Rim)

Roads:
The roads are all paved. There's an extremely good and frequent shuttle bus service.

Zion National Park, Utah

Whereas the Grand Canyon is so immense that you can see for miles; Zion is more enclosed and narrow. I'm not sure if that's the correct word to describe this stunning park but, coming straight from the Grand Canyon, that's how it felt. Looking up to the sandstone cliffs towering above you, it's easy to imagine the mountain lions which roam here. Zion is a hiker's paradise with canyons, trails and the Narrows, a gorge carved out by the Virgin River.

Camping:

Zion has three campgrounds: South, Watchman and Lava Point. Watchman Campsite is a short distance from the South Entrance. This where we set up our tent and glad that we did; it was an idyllic setting.

Roads:

Tourist numbers have increased dramatically and, therefore the National Park Service are trying to reduce the amount of traffic entering Zion. The Seasonal Shuttle bus is free and an excellent service. Parking is also limited in Zion, so getting around the park is best done with this free service.

Death Valley, Nevada & California

There seems to be a lot of places in Death Valley which sound fatal or 'dark'. Badlands Loop, Desolation Canyon, Last Chance Canyon and Furnace Creek. I can understand the name, Furnace Creek, as Death Valley is the hottest place on Earth. I'm sure there's a valid reason for the other names, but we found the park full of colour and life; not to mention lots of people! Scenic and colourful Death Valley may be, it's also a harsh and unforgiving land. A clue to this is all the safety warnings on the website and within the park, itself.

Camping:
During the summer months, there are limited campgrounds open. This is due to the extreme temperatures. However, from October to April, finding a campsite is easier. That said, we arrived in March during the Super Bloom and an Art Festival and couldn't find a suitable tent site.

Roads:
Spoilt for choice, there are more than 300 miles of paved roads, 300 miles of improved dirt roads and hundreds of miles of primitive dirt roads.

Lynn Aitken

Yosemite, California

A beautiful valley of waterfalls, meadows and granite rock formations. We visited Yosemite in March when the waterfalls were full of snow melt; a spectacular sight. This is, without a doubt, one of the most scenic parks in America and also, one of the most visited. Although we were there in springtime, I was amazed at how busy it was and could only imagine the numbers of people flocking there during the summer.

Camping:
Some of the campgrounds in Yosemite operate a *reservation only* system. However, even the first-come, *first-served* campgrounds fill up early in the day, especially from April through to September.

Roads:
Entrances into the park are via Highways 41,140 and 120. Driving in and around Yosemite is possible, weather permitting. Again, there is the ever trusty shuttle bus service.

Sequoia and Kings Canyon, California

Sitting beside each other, these two parks offer mountains, canyons and, of course, the largest trees in the world; the Sequoia

Camping:.
There are 14 campgrounds, three of which are open all year-round.

Roads:
From Fresno, Highway 180 heads east to Kings Canyon National Park, continuing on for a further 30 miles to Cedar Grove.
Driving to Sequoia from Visalia on Highway 198 via Three Rivers. Highway 198 changes to Generals Highway once in the park.

Redwood National and State Parks, Northern California and Oregon

325 miles north of San Francisco, the Redwood Parks are home to ancient coastal redwoods. The tallest trees in the world thrive here partly due to the fog rolling in from the ocean. The cooling blanket of moisture penetrates down to the forest floor; a source of water especially during the hot, dry summer.

Camping:
There's only four developed campgrounds and it's vital to make reservations to guarantee a tent site.
For *backcountry* camping, there are seven campsites.

Roads:
The most popular route through the parks is along Highway 101 between Crescent City and Orick. There are many other scenic roads, paved and unpaved, along rugged coastline and open prairies.

Glacier National Park, Montana

This is a land of glaciers, as the name suggests. The sad fact is that, one day, Glacier National Park may not have any glaciers left. In 1966, there were 35 active glaciers; in 2015, only 26 remain. What happened? We happened. Hopefully it's not too late for us to listen to what nature is trying to tell us.

Camping:
The majority of campgrounds in Glacier are *first-come, first-served*. There are, however, campgrounds which can be reserved in advance.

Roads:
During the summer the park is busy! Parking is limited but there's always the free shuttle to get around. A popular scenic drive is *Going-To-The-Sun Road*. Stretching 50 miles and crossing the Continental Divide at Logan Pass, the road offers views of mountains, waterfalls, glaciers and valleys

Denali, Alaska

Six million acres of wild and tranquil landscape from mountains to tundra. An interesting amphibian living in Denali is a type of *wood frog*. During the winter, it freezes solid; the heart stops and so does the breathing. When spring comes around, the frog thaws out and hops away!

Camping:
Denali has six campgrounds. Reservations can be made in advance for four of the sites. Igloo Creek and Sanctuary River, however, are *first-come, first-served*.

Driving:
Denali Park Road at 92 miles long, is the only road in the park. During the summer, 15 miles of the road is accessible to private vehicles as far as Savage River.
Weather permitting, Mount Denali can be seen after 9 miles along the road.

Saguaro National Park, Arizona

Named after the giant saguaro cacti, the park is separated into two areas by the city of Tucson and surrounded by mountains. The Rincon District in the east and the Tucson District to the west. The park offers protection to all types of cacti growing here.

Known as the *Kings of the Sonoran Desert*, the saguaro cacti can live longer than 200 years and grow to more than 40 feet tall.

Camping:
At present, there are six campgrounds within the Saguaro Wilderness Area and permits are required.

Roads:
In the *Rincon Mountain District*, the Cactus Forest Loop Drive is a paved road with plenty places to pull over and enjoy the views.
The *Tucson Mountain District* has an unpaved loop drive; the Bajada.

CANADA'S NATIONAL PARKS

As of 2019, Canada has 48 national parks. We were lucky to visit three of them. Breathtakingly beautiful, the parks take in mountains, vast plains and Great Lakes. As well as the countryside, for me, it was the wildlife we were seeing that I have the fondest memories of.

Banff National Park

Founded in 1885 and named after the town of Banff in Scotland, this is Canada's first national park.
The quaint resort town of Banff, is the highest town in Canada. The peaks of Mount Rundle and Mount Cascade standing watch over Banff.

Jasper National Park

The park is perfect for outdoor enthusiasts, whether it's hiking, skiing, kayaking or watching wildlife. As with every other national park, this is about protecting the fragile ecosystems and, at the same time, for us to connect with the nature within the parks.
Tha alpine town of Jasper is ideally situated for exploring the Rockies.
Jasper and Banff are completely different from each other. Whilst Banff is *picture postcard* pretty and filled with tourists, Jasper is more like an everyday community.

Kluane National Park

Heading west from Whitehorse in the Yukon, is Kluane National Park. Standing at 19,551 feet, Mount Logan, Canada's

highest mountain sits within Kluane.
The village of Haines Junction is a perfect gateway to the park and an ideal base for exploring the rugged wilderness.

Printed in Great Britain
by Amazon

79921864R00174